Nick Barber, Edinburgh. 15.1.07   £1·00

THE PARADOX OF SELF-DENIAL

W ARTRO EVANS

The Paradox
of Self-Denial

LONDON
STUART & WATKINS

FIRST PUBLISHED IN 1967
© VINCENT STUART & JOHN M WATKINS LTD
45 LOWER BELGRAVE STREET
LONDON SW1

PRINTED AND BOUND IN GREAT BRITAIN
BY ROBERT CUNNINGHAM & SONS LTD
LONGBANK WORKS, ALVA
CLACKMANNANSHIRE
SCOTLAND

SBN 7224 ·0098 5

Contents

Acknowledgments

FOR permission to use quotations from the following works, grateful acknowledgments and thanks are extended to the authors and publishers:

George Allen & Unwin Ltd: *How To Know God, The Aphorisms of Patanjali*. Translated with a New Commentary by Swami Prabhavananda and Christopher Isherwood.

Hutchinson Publishing Group Ltd: *The Psychological Attitude of Early Buddhist Philosophy, Foundations of Tibetan Mysticism*, both by Lama Anagarika Govinda. (Rider & Company, London and E. P. Dutton & Co. Inc, New York.) *The Heart of Buddhist Meditation*, by Nyanaponika Thera. (Rider & Company, London and E. P. Dutton & Co. Inc, New York.)

Hodder and Stoughton Ltd: *The Psychology of Man's Possible Evolution*, by P. D. Ouspensky.

John Murray: *The Sayings of Lao Tzu*, translated by Lionel Giles.

Vincent Stuart & John M. Watkins Ltd: *Bhagavad Gita, The Songs of the Master*. Translated with an Introduction and Commentary by Charles Johnston.

Society for Promoting Christian Knowledge (S.P.C.K.): *An Introduction to the Books of the Old Testament*, by W. O. E. Oesterley and Theodore H. Robinson.

I

Self-Delusion

FEW people find happiness although they are constantly seeking it.

Many try to find it along the road of self-gratification, but this always leads to more unhappiness, because self-gratification gives the illusion of happiness only for a while, and quickly passes away.

There are so many obstacles to self-gratification, and the struggle to overcome them is itself an obstacle to happiness. The more one strives for self-gratification, the more numerous the obstacles which have to be overcome, and the attempt to overcome all the obstacles to self-gratification, instead of bringing happiness nearer, drives it further away.

The desire for self-gratification is based on a common delusion: that there exists a self to be gratified.

This delusion that there is a self separate from all others is based on bodily sensations, with their reactions of feelings and emotions, and on the memory of past reactions. These reactions are pleasant, painful or indifferent.

The deep-rooted desire for pleasant rather than painful reactions produces a self-centred attitude to life.

From this self-centred attitude spring the seven deadly sins which are the most common symptoms of delusion.

The antidote to self-seeking is self-forgetfulness.

* * *

Happiness and unhappiness do not come from outside our own being: they are self-created.

Each man creates his own world, his own heaven and his own hell.

As long as a man's eyes are fixed upon himself, so long will he find himself in conflict with life: his desire for a personal happiness will always deprive him of it.

All desire for personal happiness comes from the animal soul within man, the primitive mind always moved to self-preservation.

Man, at this stage of development, behaves like an animal in the jungle, seeking his prey. He moves alone, like an owl or a panther, alert and ruthless. His prey is personal happiness.

He pounces on happiness greedily, but he is constantly glancing over his shoulder. His happiness, even at its highest point, is overshadowed by fear.

What he has seized for his own enjoyment can always be taken away from him by men like himself, or by the ever-changing conditions in which he finds himself. He has to deal not only with people, but also with the unpredictable course of events.

Fear is his greatest enemy.

Man cannot find enduring happiness until he overcomes fear.

*   *   *

There are many forms of fear, but they all spring from the same delusion: the belief in a separate self which must at all costs be preserved.

This concept of a separate self or personality divides men against each other, and sets man in conflict with his environment.

There is also the fear of fear itself.

The memory of the almost overwhelming force of past fears

2

strengthens the fear of present and future demands upon one's resources.

The fear of being unable to control and to conceal fear is the worst fear of all.

The concept of a unique, separate ego or self can be maintained undisturbed only in a state of complete isolation, or in a small community of people entirely dependent on, and subservient to, that ego.

Such a state of isolation or of domination over others could be achieved by one willing to live in extreme poverty the life of a hermit, or by a person of great wealth.

The purpose of such isolation or domination over others is self-preservation: to withdraw oneself from all attempts to remove one's attention from oneself, and from all intrusions into one's self-absorption.

Man's inclination to isolation and self-absorption is one of the chief causes of unhappiness.

One cannot hope to overcome this inclination until one sees clearly that the state of self-absorption is a state of delusion.

*　　*　　*

The desire to fix the attention entirely on the self, and the necessity to remove it for long periods and fix it on what is considered as not-self, i.e. other people and matters connected with other people, induce a hidden conflict in the mind. This conflict or clash of interests is the cause of fatigue, of nervous strain, and of fear.

The cause of every negative thought is self-concern, and until one is free of self-concern, there can be no enduring happiness or peace of mind.

The desire and the will to be rid of self-concern is the first step that must be taken to achieve this happiness. Then the way is open for the practice of self-denial.

Self-denial means removing one's attention completely from the self with its desires and aversions, and fixing it constantly, by a resolute effort of will, upon what is not-self, i.e. on other people and matters connected with other people.

Every moment that is free of self-concern is a moment of happiness.

The mind cannot be occupied with two objects of a completely opposite content at one and the same time, so that the way to keep the attention off oneself is to fix it on what is not-self; on anything that does not inspire desire or aversion.

Self-denial is the process of passing from a primitive state of consciousness to the freedom of a more enlightened attitude towards people and events.

The primitive attitude is one of self-interest and self-concern. Everything that occurs is viewed from the standpoint of personal feelings and emotions, translated into desire or aversion, greed or hatred. This state of consciousness was the natural reaction of primitive man to the conditions in which he had to struggle for survival. Modern man has inherited this attitude from his forbears, and until he understands that it is no longer relevant to his own condition, he remains a savage.

Greed and hatred turn men into monsters, and cannot bring happiness.

*   *   *

Self-denial cannot be properly achieved without grasping the truth that it means the denial of the existence of self. It is essential to understand what the so-called self or ego is composed of, and that it is a delusion.

The concept of selfhood springs from man's identification of

4

himself with his own body, with his sensations, feelings and emotions, and with his memories, both painful and pleasant. His memories colour his present and his future. Animated by greed for pleasant sensations and hatred for the unpleasant, his purpose separates him in his own mind from all other men.

The first step to take in freeing the mind from this delusion is to remember that all men have separate bodies, which through the five senses, give them various sensations which in turn induce feelings and emotions. Greed and hatred are the automatic reactions to pleasant and painful sensations. Basically, every man's notion of his own separate existence springs from his own consciousness, and this notion is common to all men. In fact, there is very little difference, at this stage of development, between one ego and another, between the innumerable selves that occupy innumerable separate bodies.

To claim uniqueness for one's own state of consciousness, and to erect the sum total of memories, sensations, feelings and emotions into a separate ego, self or personality to be asserted and defended against all others, is as absurd as to consider one's own feet to be more important than anyone else's feet, or to say that one's own nose has a greater claim to consideration than every other nose in existence.

One could go so far as to say that, at bottom, there is only one man, and that every man is only a copy of that man, with certain superficial modifications due to the action of experience or environment inducing varying interpretations of life.

The body and the mind are instruments of consciousness, which is an attribute of the life that animates them, but as long as the mind remains in the delusion of selfhood, moved alternately by greed or hatred, there is no possibility of growth. Until this delusion is removed, there can only be separation, conflict, division and unhappiness.

* * *

To understand the delusion of selfhood does not automatically set one free from its domination. Longstanding habits of thought are not easily cast aside. There must be re-training of the mind to form new attitudes based on a new outlook and a deeper understanding of life.

If this training of the mind is to succeed, each day must become a day of self-observation, when every impulse of self-concern is recognized for what it is, and is immediately rejected. It takes time to form the habit of self-examination in the midst of the unavoidable distractions of daily life, when the ever-changing circumstances and unexpected events continually provide an incentive to greed or hatred. In contact with the habitual self-assertion of others, the former attitude of self-concern is not easily suppressed.

It is, therefore, essential that some portion of each day should be spent in reminding oneself that self-concern springs from the delusion of selfhood. If this thought is daily reaffirmed, there will come a gradual transformation of attitude, as impersonal as the former attitude was personal. People and events will be seen as they are, no longer distorted by the spectacles of self-interest.

To know oneself and to understand one's own delusions is to understand, and make allowances for, the behaviour of others. Then one can see clearly that the whole philosophy of worldliness springs from the delusion of selfhood, expressing itself as desire and aversion, greed and hatred. The reactions of pleasure and pain are the source of desire, which governs man's behaviour throughout life. Aversion is the negative side of desire, being the desire to avoid pain.

The term 'pleasure' may include anything from the mildest sense of enjoyment or well-being to the most intense states of sensual or mental gratification, and the term 'pain' covers everything from the most trivial worry or inconvenience to the acutest physical or mental agony.

Desire takes various forms, but the excessive indulgence of any desire brings into operation the limiting factor of fatigue, and of the consequent loss of efficiency in the body, the organ or instrument of consciousness.

Being able to record experience in his memory, and to reflect upon it, the mind of man is also able to distinguish between a moderate and immoderate indulgence of his desires. His negative desire to avoid pain helps to control his positive desire to enjoy pleasure.

It is by the practice of reflection upon his own experience, and upon the experience of others, that the mind of man acquires self-knowledge. The pleasure of avoiding pain through self-knowledge gives him a feeling of mastery, and increases his desire for self-knowledge.

This desire in time broadens and deepens into a desire for an all-inclusive knowledge and understanding of absolute truth and reality. From this desire springs every philosophy and theory of life, and all religious doctrines have the same source.

2

Desire and Aversion

MAN's development is the development of his mind, which, by the practice of reflection, grows conscious not only of effects but also of causes. His desire to avoid pain impels him to seek and understand its cause.

Pain may be defined as the absence of tranquillity, and is the antithesis of pleasure. It manifests itself as a multitude of effects, each of which has to be studied in order to determine its cause. When the effect has been traced back to its source, it is found that desire, whether satisfied or unsatisfied, is the cause of pain.

Some forms of bodily suffering, it is true, cannot be attributed entirely to desire, because they are due to the natural deterioration of the physical organism, but this deterioration which comes with age can be accelerated by self-indulgence. A great deal of suffering has its origin in failure to control the appetites.

Satisfied desire can be the cause of pain in three ways:

1. When the object of desire has been obtained, there comes the fear of losing it.
2. When pleasure is enjoyed, it cannot remain indefinitely an object of attention: the consciousness of pleasure, having attained its full strength, diminishes in intensity, and gradually fades away, giving place to new desires and to other objects of attention.
3. The satisfaction of desire is frequently marred by a sense of guilt, and by anxiety about its consequences.

8

Unsatisfied desire, likewise, causes pain because the desire persists, and its frustration gives rise to hatred of the obstacle to its satisfaction.

The satisfaction of desire strengthens desire, the experience of pleasure being always accompanied by its corresponding re-actions of pain. Moved by desire, the mind finds itself con-stantly in one of these alternate states of pleasure or pain.

Desire itself, as it arises, disturbs the tranquillity of the mind, giving rise to anxiety as to the probability of its satisfaction, and hatred for possible obstacles. Tranquillity may also be dis-turbed by doubt whether the pleasure to be derived from the satisfaction of desire can justify the necessary expenditure of energy and the inevitable consequence of pain.

The memory of past suffering often causes a change of desire: the desire to avoid suffering becomes stronger than the desire for pleasure. Thus self-control, or the control of desire, is the sub-stitution of one desire for another. One need not follow certain courses of action in order to learn that they lead inevitably to suffering: one has only to observe the sufferings of those who have already followed such courses of action. It is thus possible to learn from the experience of those who have failed to learn from experience.

But even when the desire to avoid suffering becomes stronger than the desire for pleasure, one cannot avoid the suffering of foregoing the pleasure. To abstain from pleasure in order to avoid pain is itself painful. The desire to avoid pain is also a source of pain.

The positive side of desire is to enjoy pleasure, its negative side to avoid pain. Yet the negative desire to avoid pain is also a positive desire to enjoy the pleasure of avoiding pain. Thus every desire is both positive and negative, and is, therefore, a source of conflict. One cannot satisfy the positive and negative side of any desire at one and the same time: a choice has to be made. The moment of choice is also the moment of renunciation, and renunciation is suffering.

Desire is conflict and is in itself both pleasure and pain.

The life of desire based on sense-impressions with their reactions of feelings and emotions, is a succession of continually changing states of consciousness. Desire itself also changes into satiety, disgust and loathing.

Objects of desire become less desirable, and finally cease to attract. They are displaced by other objects: there is always something to be desired, some evil to be resisted. For desire, at this level of consciousness, is also aversion.

It is desire aroused by sense-impressions, feelings and emotions, coloured by memory, which separates the mind, at this stage of development, from its object of perception, and gives man the sense of individual and separate existence. Thus the ego or human personality in its most limited form becomes aware of itself.

Pain and suffering impel man to reflection upon his experience, and to trace every adverse event back to its source. When he reaches the stage of development in which he is capable of objective reflection and self-observation, he discovers that desire based on sense-impressions, feelings and emotions, coloured by memory, is the source of pain.

It is clear that an enlargement of consciousness has taken place when the mind is able to observe the self which has identified itself with desire. A new self or ego thus comes into being, which must, to some extent, be independent of sense-impressions, feelings and emotions, in that it is able to dissociate itself from them.

Each self is a state of consciousness: the state of the consciousness of desire and of the consequences of desire, grows into the state of consciousness which accepts desire and aversion as the automatic and instinctive reactions of the undeveloped mind. This is a new state of consciousness produced by the experience of life: it is mind widening and deepening its field of vision.

This developing mind with its enlarged field of consciousness is animated by a new desire: to set itself free from desire and aversion, from greed and hatred. This desire can only survive the resistance of the old self, the expression and embodiment of delusion, if it is based on strong conviction, and pursued with unwavering resolution. The habit of yielding to every desire must be replaced by the habit of alert, disillusioned scrutiny, discouraging, controlling and subduing every desire based on sense-impressions with their reactions of greed and hatred.

* * *

Reflection upon one's own experience should, at this stage of the mind's development, be extended to include the experience and conclusions of other minds. No man is alone in his struggle for freedom from delusion: many others have gone through this painful process before, and have recorded their convictions in writing. All mystical literature, including the sacred Scriptures of many ancient religions, offer him, in memorable and beautiful phrases, the assurance which he needs.

But he must not confuse reading with reflection; he must beware of the temptation to accept without question everything he reads in books. Different teachers approach the truth from different directions, and sometimes stop short of the truth itself, contenting themselves with naming the symptoms of error, and advocating the practice of certain virtues as antidotes for specific vices.

The assurance which is offered to man in mystical literature, and in the sacred Scriptures of ancient religions, is that freedom from pain and suffering can be obtained. They provide him with food for thought, but he must, by constant reflection, discover the way for himself.

The mind is the focus of a succession of moments of consciousness dependent on sense-impressions or memory-impressions, which cause reactions of pleasure or pain, or else a neutral reaction, a simple awareness, devoid of pleasure and pain. The reaction of pleasure provokes a deeper reaction consisting of the pleasurableness of pleasure: and the reaction of pain a deeper reaction consisting of the painfulness of pain.

These deeper reactions are the cause of desire and aversion.

The error into which man has fallen is to identify himself with these contrasting and vivid states of consciousness, and to build on these shifting sands the elaborate edifice of a permanent ego, self or personality, which, with the passage of Time, and the accumulation of reactions, becomes a stronghold for self-assertion. The identification of these accumulated reactions to innumerable moments of consciousness with a self or ego claiming as a right the constant enjoyment of pleasure and immunity from pain, is a delusion.

Those vivid and sharply defined moments of consciousness experienced as pleasure or pain are as impersonal as the intervening moments of consciousness with their neutral reactions devoid of pleasure and pain.

In the neutral states of consciousness, devoid of pleasure and pain, desire and aversion are absent; and when these are absent, man is hardly aware of a self or ego. Similarly, when the mind is entirely concentrated on study or work, there is often complete self-forgetfulness: the mind is aware only of the object of attention.

When desire and aversion are regarded as impersonal positive and negative reactions to the impact of experience, and self-identification with them as a delusion, their elimination will be far easier than when this identification is regarded as real. So many thinkers are content to advocate the suppression of desire as the remedy for suffering, but so long as this self-identification with desire persists, the suppression of desire will itself be a cause of suffering. The true remedy is to recognize that desire and aversion are transient states of consciousness to be observed with an impersonal detachment as automatic reactions to sense and memory impressions, and that they do not constitute a self or ego. Then they will lose their former status and importance, and can be set aside or ignored with equanimity. The delusion of self-identification will be known to be the reflection of an 'unconscious' state of consciousness.

3

The Awakened Mind

THE 'unconscious' state of consciousness is described in the New Testament as 'death' or 'sleep'. To the disciple who wanted first to bury his father, Jesus said: 'Follow me, and let the dead bury their dead.' *Matthew* viii.22.

In the Epistle to the Ephesians, v.14, we read: 'Awake, thou that sleepest, and arise from the dead, and Christ shall give thee light.'

Ouspensky calls this state 'waking sleep' or 'relative' consciousness. 'It is useful to remember that this is the inner meaning of many ancient doctrines. The best known to us is Christianity, in which the idea that men live in sleep and must first of all awake, is the basis of all the explanations of human life, although it is very rarely understood as it should be understood, in this case literally.' P. D. Ouspensky: *The Psychology of Man's Possible Evolution.* (Hodder & Stoughton, London.)

In Buddhist psychology, this state is described thus: 'With reference to the goal of deliverance, two main modes of consciousness can be distinguished: the directed and the undirected ... Undirected consciousness ... allows itself to be driven hither and thither by instinct-born motives and external impressions.' Lama Anagarika Govinda: *The Psychological Attitude of Early Buddhist Philosophy.* (Rider & Company, London.)

'Unconscious' consciousness is the condition in which man is aware of his environment, and of himself as being separate from it. He is aware of his reactions to his environment, and of his desires and aversions: his existence is a struggle to control his

14

environment, and to bring it into harmony with his desire for pleasant sensations. This he cannot do for any length of time because it is continually changing, nor can he control the desires and aversions of others, who, being in the same state as himself, cause it to change.

Thus egoism, or the illusion of an unchanging selfhood, always in conflict with a constantly changing environment, produces constant suffering.

Suffering teaches those who are capable of reflection on experience and of learning from it, that egoism is the automatic and mechanical reaction of 'unconscious' consciousness, and this is the first step in the awakening of consciousness, when consciousness becomes conscious of itself.

When man is able to recognize the self or ego as a delusion, and that desire and aversion are no more than a desperate attempt to preserve this delusion, he is entering the state of 'conscious' consciousness. He then begins to understand that it is not in his environment that he will find what he seeks, i.e. a sense of inner harmony in relation to it, but in his own consciousness.

'Conscious' consciousness is an attempt to discover a new, and more satisfactory interpretation of a man's relation to his environment. The old interpretation of a permanent ego or self constantly demanding, as of right, the ceaseless enjoyment of pleasure and immunity from pain, having been discarded, a new answer must be found. Life cannot be lived without a purpose: the discovery of a new interpretation of experience thus becomes the purpose of an awakened or 'conscious' consciousness.

The mind in the state of conscious consciousness will observe that the old egocentric attitude is very tenacious. But the constant effort of alert concentration required to recognize and subdue it will bring its own reward, and will lead gradually to a deeper insight. For the elimination of desire and aversion, the suppression of the delusive self or ego, form the negative aspect of a larger purpose, the positive aspect of which becomes known only when its negative aspect is being fulfilled. The seeker after Truth must proceed from the known to the unknown, and fresh glimpses and further understanding are given to him who acts faithfully upon what has already been understood.

This larger purpose is nothing less than the development of the intuitive or cosmic consciousness, in which there is no separation between man and his environment, between subject and object, between the knower and the known.

In the first stages of conscious consciousness, however, the mind is groping its way slowly out of the darkness of delusion, and has no conception of what the light into which it is entering will ultimately reveal. It is sufficiently occupied in observing the persistence of delusion, and in restraining the ego in its constant struggle for self-assertion. From time to time, the temptation to give way to egoistic habits and attitudes of long standing will be very strong, and sometimes the mind will be assailed by doubts about the validity of its own conclusions.

Every victory over the delusive self, however, gives renewed conviction and strength of purpose: there comes, after each successful effort, a feeling of self-mastery and freedom. The dismissal of desire and aversion as impersonal and transient movements of consciousness brings tranquillity: the mind is no longer the plaything of fortuitous circumstance. Avoidance of action to satisfy desire and aversion prevents further entanglements in the self-created world of illusion.

'Conscious' consciousness is, therefore, a selective consciousness: it is no longer a matter of automatic, mechanical or habitual reactions to sense and memory impressions, to feelings and emotions. On the contrary, it is a conscious and deliberate self-detachment from the effects of consciousness, and a fundamental change of attitude.

Having rejected the old, superficial, egoistic interpretation of experience, the mind becomes more impersonal. Desire and aversion are seen, as it were, from a safe distance, to be examined at leisure, and not as matters of immediate consequence. There are fewer hasty and impetuous actions, a growing preference for silence rather than speech, and a conviction of the relative unimportance of events. The removal of self-concern brings unconcern and indifference to the mind.

This tranquillity, however, can only be maintained as long as the concept of an unchanging ego or self is recognized at all times as a delusion, and this calls for an untiring control of consciousness. Thus conscious consciousness is the process of the gradual depersonalization of consciousness: the mind deliberately withdraws its attention from the reactions of desire and aversion, and the former separation between subject and object, between the observer and the observed, is reduced until it is finally eliminated.

When the absence of desire and aversion is recognized as a cause of tranquillity, there will arise a strong temptation to seek tranquillity for its own sake, and to make this a conscious purpose. To yield to this temptation is to fall into the old trap of egoistic desire, and to become once more entangled in the world of delusion.

Mind is the focal point of consciousness, and in the state of 'conscious' consciousness, the mind assumes control of the activities and operations of consciousness. It is the mind, therefore, that awakes out of sleep, and takes charge of the little world called man.

The essence of past experience, the memory of past suffering, become the wisdom of the mind: by its light man must find his way out of the darkness of delusion.

*   *   *

The first state of consciousness, in which the mind, the focus of consciousness, identifies itself with an unchanging ego or personality, is purely subjective. When the mind rejects this limited interpretation of experience as a delusion, consciousness becomes more and more objective.

The mind can now subject whatever comes into consciousness to an impersonal scrutiny, and so arrive at a less distorted view of life. In this state, a man may examine himself and try to understand what he is.

No longer identifying his mind with an unchanging self, it is now possible for him to identify himself with a mind that has rejected the delusion of an unchanging self or ego. The mind, and everything that comes into it, is no longer regarded as the self, but as an instrument of consciousness.

There is no longer any attempt to define the self: the word is used merely as a convenient term to express that individual awareness of experience, that sum total of cognition, feeling and volition, peculiar and distinct, which finds its focus in the mind.

The awakened mind, in the state of objective consciousness, is seeking a more satisfactory interpretation of experience to provide a new purpose to life. Its starting-point must always be the conviction that all objects of attention are to be observed without desire or aversion: there must be an unwavering resolution not to return to the bondage of self-seeking and self-love.

In the state of delusion that prevails when the mind is identified with an unchanging ego or self, man lives, as it were, in a prison of his own making, behind high walls: he can see nothing except his own desires and aversions. He is aware only of himself, and of the conflict within him. He is never really aware of other people, except when they serve his purpose or oppose his will.

When the mind is awakened out of this delusion, and becomes capable of objective consciousness, other people are seen for the first time as they really are. There comes a new and more sympathetic understanding of human behaviour and of human suffering. The gradual reduction of the preoccupations of self-love permits the growth of compassion. The prison is no longer a prison, but a house and a home: its door and windows are opened, and man goes out to meet his fellows.

The behaviour of others can now be observed with an objective detachment, and what was formerly the cause of egocentric reactions is seen as the product of delusion. This delusion, being the almost universal state of human consciousness, reveals itself in its true character to the awakened mind of the man who has reached the state of conscious objective consciousness even more clearly in others than in himself. Whatever doubts he may have had before, the irrational conduct of men, both singly and in the mass, can only be ascribed to their false belief in a non-existent, unchanging ego, whose desires and aversions, being regarded as matters of paramount importance, invariably make for greed and hatred.

Understanding the nature of this delusion, the awakened man is better able to avoid becoming involved in the delusions of others. At the same time, with the growth of objective consciousness, he becomes increasingly aware of the universal suffering caused by this one delusion, and is moved by compassion.

As self-love moves a man to action on behalf of self, so compassion brings to mind the desire to help others. Thus, although he himself may avoid suffering by the consistent suppression of desire and aversion, he shares the sufferings of those who are still the slaves of delusion. Not only that, for the delusions of mankind have far-reaching consequences which affect the enlightened as well as the deluded.

The awakened man, observing his own state of consciousness with objective detachment, learns that compassion unites him with others. Observing his fellow-men without self-concern, he sees in all his former delusive self. This recognition of the relationship of man to man is revealed by the removal of the delusion of separation which is the negative side of the positive delusion of an independent ego or personality. Reality is hidden by the veils of ignorance, but is always there. When error is deleted, the mind is conscious of what is, without knowing, possibly, at the time, that what it is conscious of is Reality.

In this new state of enlightenment, human life is seen as a dream, in which men move like automatons in the sleep of delusion. Innumerable unawakened minds, governed by the universal illusion of separation, react continuously upon each other, always binding mankind more and more tightly in the bonds of greed and hatred.

The removal of the delusion of separation brings the awakened mind closer to the deluded, and this sense of unity is seen as revealing the true nature of consciousness: that it is a quality of Life itself, and that its inherent properties and potentialities are available to all who possess life. There is only one life and only one consciousness. Before they can be examined objectively, the veils of delusion must be torn aside. Then only can the reality of life be seen and understood.

4

Impersonal Consciousness

IMPERSONAL consciousness is the state in which the mind penetrates the delusion of personality, and sees, behind every appearance of individuality, the impersonal Life Force animating all beings, and endowing all with the faculty of consciousness.

The world of man is seen as a self-created illusion, existing only in the elementary and limited consciousness of unawakened minds, reacting automatically to sense-and-memory impressions, to deeply implanted habits of thought and inherited delusions. In the centre of this world is the self-created ego or personality, fighting desperately to preserve its existence of separate individuality from encroachment. The unreality of almost every aspect of human life springs from the basic delusion of personality.

It follows, also, that all the sins of which man is guilty have the same character of unreality: pride, envy, anger, covetousness, sloth, gluttony and lust have no real existence. They are only the symptoms of a deep-rooted delusion, and as such, they are equally delusions.

When the cancerous growth of personality is removed, and its tenacious desires and aversions eliminated, these symptoms, called the seven deadly sins, disappear. The mind is then conscious only of peace, tranquillity, and compassion. Instead of separation and conflict, there comes a sense of the oneness, of the unity, of all life.

The removal of delusion enables the mind, the focus of consciousness, to observe the character of consciousness itself, because whatever is in consciousness when all egocentric thought has been eliminated belongs to itself, and owes nothing to the human mind. Tranquillity, and compassion and love are then seen, not as the creations of the intellect, but as the properties of the impersonal consciousness of Life.

The awakened mind begins to understand that behind all phenomena as they appear in human consciousness is the Reality of the invisible, conscious life Force, sustaining and permeating all beings, manifesting itself in an infinite variety of forms. Invisible and unknown, the conscious life Force reveals its true nature to those who will open their eyes to see it as it is.

Known or unknown, recognized or unrecognized, life reveals itself as compassion and love, constantly breaking through the mists of delusion, like rays of brilliant light piercing a black cloud, to impel the deluded to acts of unselfish service. Even those who are still in the 'unconscious' or sleep state of consciousness experience the joy of the impersonal consciousness of life in those brief, self-forgetful moments when compassion unites them with their fellows.

Thus many who retain a false belief in the separate and unchanging ego or personality unconsciously allow the compassionate impulse of life itself to direct them, and attribute this impulse to the ego itself. Under the influence of religious teachings, with their stress on self-denial and brotherly love, they will occasionally modify their habitual egocentric attitude, but only to the extent of treating such modifications as acts of the all-important ego, which, temporarily, consents to forgo its rights. In the 'sleep' state of consciousness, there is no question of taking the doctrine of self-denial literally, and every departure from the normal practice of self-assertion serves only to strengthen the ego-delusion, giving rise to self-righteousness, vanity and pride.

But once Life is seen as existing in its own right, independent and impersonal, endowing all beings with energy and the faculty of consciousness, the ego-sense dwindles in the presence of the infinite vastness of Reality now unveiling itself to the awakened mind.

On the other hand, the mind becomes aware of the vastness of the unreality in which humanity dwells, the dark self-created world of ignorance and delusion, of greed, fear and hatred, of cynicism, indifference and despair, its darkness relieved from time to time by glimpses of the ever-present joy and compassion of the impersonal consciousness of Life.

The ego-delusion separates man from man, but the impersonal consciousness of life unites men together in the bonds of compassion and love.

*   *   *

When consciousness is seen as the property of life itself, existing independently of man's delusions, it becomes clear that the consciousness of man is in the life that animates his body. Every being having life has consciousness, and this individual consciousness is but a part of what may be called 'universal consciousness'.

As life pervades every part of man's body, so consciousness pervades every part of it. The consciousness of the body has its focus in the mind, which has its own interpretation of the meaning of what it is conscious of, according to whether it is in the unawakened or the enlightened state of consciousness. This interpretation in turn pervades the consciousness of the whole body.

It must follow that the universal consciousness has its focus in what may be called the universal mind, and whatever is in that mind must be reflected throughout the universal consciousness as an integral quality of universal consciousness.

Since the life and the consciousness are one, manifesting themselves in a limitless variety of forms, it should be possible for the human mind, representing, as it does, the highest embodiment of conscious life, to discover the integral qualities of universal consciousness, and for such an important task the proper method must be found.

The method which has been adopted for centuries by all earnest seekers after Truth has been the method of meditation and contemplation. The attempt to become conscious of universal consciousness can be made only when man's normal egocentric attitude has been recognized as a delusion. Then the mind is ready to begin the practice of meditation.

For this practice it is essential to be alone in silence. All discursive thought should cease. With the eyes closed, to avoid the distractions of visible objects, one should wait and listen to the voice of the silence. The ability to do this for any length of time grows with practice, but at first it is easy to relapse into mere day-dreaming. Every idle thought, and indeed, thought of every kind, should be regarded as an interruption of the purpose of meditation, which is to wait and listen.

In this completely relaxed state of body and mind, the attempt is made to achieve an entirely new state of awareness. In the normal process of cognition, there is at all times the subject and the object, the knower and the known. There is an awareness not only of the object perceived but also of the mind perceiving the object. This process of perception is never entirely objective, because the subjective attitude of the perceiver is always interposed between the object perceived and the perceiver. In meditation, the attempt is made to eliminate every trace of subjectivity, to submerge individual consciousness entirely in the Universal Consciousness.

Such an experience, when it occurs, must be regarded as beyond description, because where there is no subjectivity there can be no objectivity, and without objectivity there is no possibility of description. When the experience itself has ceased, and finite consciousness returns once more to its normal condition, there remains only an incommunicable memory. None the less, it is possible, by the process of abstraction, to attempt a negative description: that is to say by indicating what such a state of consciousness could not contain.

The human mind is subject to the limitations of Time and Place, and also of its own physical organs of consciousness. But the Universal Mind, existing as it must, independently of its innumerable physical manifestations, must clearly be as boundless as Life itself. Since the human mind, the focus of human consciousness, is but an individualized but distorted portion of the Universal Mind, it most nearly approaches the state or condition of the whole of which it is a part when it is emptied of selfhood, of all ideas of an independent existence, and of all desire and aversion. In that state, the mind is untroubled and still, like the surface of a lake on a calm day; past and future no longer exist: there is only the timeless present.

When all other objects of attention have been removed, there remains Life itself, of which the whole physical organism becomes intensely aware, its presence being felt both within and without to the extent of the power of the attention given to it at any given moment. The Universal Consciousness, being universal, must of necessity be absolutely impersonal, available to all to the extent in which it is summoned, reflecting indifferently delusion as well as truth, completely unobtrusive and self-effacing.

The elimination of all egocentric delusion being the one essential prerequisite of the practice of meditation, it is only in

25

a state of perfect humility or humble awareness that the human mind can get to know the Universal Mind, and since the Universal Consciousness reflects faithfully whatever is presented to it, it follows that humility is the main characteristic of the Universal Mind.

* * *

Those who are not born already meek and lowly in heart can acquire the virtue of humility by the process of deliberate self-effacement, but it must be an essential quality of the Universal Consciousness, for otherwise it could not be universally available and amenable at every stage of the development of innumerable beings.

Therefore, the Universal Mind may be said to be humility itself. It is this impersonal humility of the Universal Consciousness of Life which guarantees the freedom of human consciousness.

The awakened mind, by its constant endeavour to eliminate the delusion of a permanent ego or separate personality, makes room for the growth of humility, for humility is the absence of self-assertion.

The cultivation of humility brings immediate rewards of detachment from the pressure of external events, of freedom from anxiety and self-concern, and of tranquillity in the performance of uncongenial duties. In this attitude of humble awareness, the mind becomes its own refuge, immovable in the midst of commotion.

True humility is not to be confused with the cringing self-abasement of unenlightened minds, whose servility is the product of fear and envy. The humility of the enlightened is the product of self-mastery, and is an unfailing source of wisdom and power.

26

The constant dismissal of the ego or self required by the practice of humility does not, as might be expected, produce a feeling of emptiness; on the contrary, humility itself is felt as a Presence, accompanying the humble in all his ways. Having removed self from consciousness, there is an awareness of Life as an invisible companion whose name is Humility.

Humility induces also an attitude of non-resistance to the various demands upon one's time and energy: there is a new willingness to serve and co-operate. In the company of others, there is an awareness, not only of individual delusions, but of the Universal Consciousness behind all delusion. The awakened mind is humble in the presence of the Universal Mind, and with humility comes compassion for the deluded.

Self-effacement resulting in humility invariably brings with it, not only compassion, but an awareness of compassion as a distinct and integral part of humility. The Universal Mind is compassion as well as humility, and when the barrier of self is removed, the qualities of the Universal Consciousness reveal themselves to the enlightened or awakened human mind.

The removal of the barrier of self in one man helps to lower the barrier of self in others: the light of humility and compassion, breaking through the veils of delusion, reveals the same light hidden in the life of all men. It is the light of the Universal Mind shining in the Universal Consciousness.

Humility is the highest form of wisdom, being based on freedom from delusion, so that the willingness to serve and to co-operate with others never becomes an indiscriminate compliance with the requests of the deluded. Insight into the nature of human delusions and compassion for suffering humanity counterbalance each other.

Pain being man's most effective teacher, it must always be a matter for careful consideration to what extent others should be assisted to evade the consequences of their own actions: such assistance, if given before the lesson of experience has been properly understood, may well be a hindrance to another's development. Humility guides the awakened mind in making the right choice between action and inaction. True compassion often lies in non-interference. No-one can ever be really helped until he is ready to abandon his delusions.

The attitude of humility is a sure safeguard against complacency and spiritual pride, for the delusion of a permanent unchanging ego or self is hard to destroy, and may assume many different forms. When the mind is awakened, and begins to understand the nature of human delusions, care must be taken not to identify this new insight with a more subtle ego or self of superior intelligence, thus forming a new barrier of self-importance and a fresh delusion of separation.

The practice of humility gradually transforms the character of the awakened man, so that its unusual quality becomes apparent to those best able to observe his manner of life. Character is the reflection of the various attitudes of mind which are translated into outward behaviour, and a close observation of behaviour reveals the predominating attitudes of mind.

Until the mind is awakened, the attitudes which it adopts remain unobserved, and there is no possibility of a conscious direction of behaviour. But even the unawakened mind can observe the behaviour of the awakened man, and by seeking to understand the cause of his tranquillity, may itself be awakened.

Humility not only transforms the character of the humble, but also changes the character of every situation in which humility is present. Offering no resistance to self-assertion, the self-assertion of others fades away, and every situation being met by an attitude of non-resistance, is seen as it really is.

The words which are used to describe the various attitudes of the human mind can evoke those attitudes, and by frequently repeating the word that describes a desired attitude, that attitude can become habitual.

Words have life and power, and by concentrating deeply upon the meaning of a word, one can assume a conscious direction of behaviour. The word 'humility' often repeated fills the mind with its essence, and leaves little room for the attempted encroachment of the all-too-persistent self.

Thus, by the cultivation of humility, the awakened man may set himself free from the burdens of self-assertion. He withdraws from the conflicts of the worldly scene, and becomes an observer of the movements of consciousness: avoiding at all times the pitfall of self-reference, he detaches his mind from the net of human entanglements. He directs his behaviour in accordance with a definite purpose.

In the state of delusion there is no conscious purpose: what appears to be purpose is no more than an automatic reaction to sensation, expressing itself as desire and aversion, greed and hatred. But the awakened mind is no longer misled by this reaction, which is clearly seen as the cause of suffering.

The elimination of desire and aversion is the negative aspect of a conscious purpose: the positive aspect is to achieve enlightenment and liberation; it is to know God, 'in knowledge of whom standeth our eternal life, whose service is perfect freedom'. 'The Collect for Peace.' *The Book of Common Prayer*. It is to reach that state of illumination in which the soul's aspiration is that 'among the sundry and manifold changes of the world, our hearts may surely there be fixed, where true joys are to be found'. 'The Collect for the Fourth Sunday after Easter.' *The Book of Common Prayer*.

Joy, for the unawakened mind, is the satisfaction of desire, but this cannot endure in a state of constant self-concern. The fulness of joy can only be found in the absence of conflict, when the struggle to perpetuate the ego-delusion has been abandoned. Man's heaviest burden is the self, and until he is rid of it, he cannot hope for any enduring peace or happiness.

This, then, is the way to the fulness of joy: to seek for no personal satisfaction, to be without self-seeking. Such a state of non-attachment can only be attained as the result of a conscious purpose to attain it, and that purpose must never be allowed to waver for one moment. For this reason, it is essential that no association or relationship should be formed which could in any way hinder its fulfilment.

Such a conscious purpose is, therefore, a complete dedication to a way of life which is at the same time a way of death: the death of the ego or self, the end of planning for oneself, the end of self-centred hopes and aims, the end of striving and struggling.

To maintain such a purpose for any length of time, there must be a daily and hourly recognition of it as the true purpose of one's life. Periods set aside for meditation must begin with the conscious acceptance of it. Books should be read which extol this purpose, so that the mind may become one with it. Every thought and every act must accord with it, so that no room can be found for any other purpose.

This resolute watchfulness will in time become a habit as difficult to shake off as the old habit of self-assertion. A new attitude to life will be formed.

5

The Inheritance of the Meek

EVERY religion is both an interpretation, and a way, of life. The paradox of self-denial is a fundamental doctrine common to all religions.

With the exception of Buddhism, religion consists in the recognition of the Universal Mind as God, the Absolute Good, the Supreme Arbiter of human destiny. It follows, of necessity, that man's relationship to God must be one of meekness and humility. But while the Buddha declined to formulate any metaphysical doctrines for his followers, he insisted that the Clear Comprehension of Reality, or Non-delusion, reveals that there is no permanent self or ego, and this truth is contained in the fundamental doctrine of Anatta or Impersonality.

The Hindu religion also teaches the non-existence of the self: 'The mind is able to perceive because it reflects both the Atman and the objects of perception. The individual soul is known to Hindu philosophy as the "reflected" or the "shadow" Atman. It has no separate existence. It is only the reflection of the Atman upon the mind, which gives rise to a separate sense of ego.' 'How To Know God'. *The Yoga Aphorisms of Patanjali*. Translated with a New Commentary by Swami Prabhavananda and Christopher Isherwood. (George Allen & Unwin.)

The *Bhagavad Gita*, the Gospel of Hinduism, teaches that the illumined renounces self, and devotes his life to the worship of the Atman, the indwelling Godhead:

'Arjuna said: What is the description of one firm in perception, of one firm in soul-vision. O thou of the flowing hair? He

31

who is firm in soul, how does he speak? How does he sit? How does he go?

'The Master said: When he offers up all desires that dwell in the heart, O son of Pritha, in soul rejoicing in the Soul, then he is said to be firm in perception.' *Bhagavad Gita*. The Songs of the Master. Translated with an Introduction and Commentary by Charles Johnston. (Vincent Stuart & John M. Watkins Ltd. London.)

Similarly, the Taoist philosophers of China stress the importance of humility and self-denial. Lao Tzu, a forerunner of Confucius, wrote in his 'Tao Te Ching': 'Therefore the Sage embraces Unity, and is a model for all under Heaven. He is free from self-display, therefore he shines forth . . . Inasmuch as he does not strive, there is no one in the world who can strive with him.' *The Sayings of Lao Tzu*. Translated by Lionel Giles. (John Murray, London.)

Although it is possible by the practice of reflection to arrive at the truth of the non-existence of a permanent ego, and by constant effort, to overcome greed and hatred, yet, for the majority, it is easier to achieve self-denial by affirming the existence of God as the Source and Sustainer of all conscious life, and to place obedience to the Universal Mind as the starting-point of all activity. This attitude is the foundation of all religions except Buddhism, and is the essential message of their sacred Scriptures. For the Western mind, whose development has been deeply influenced by Christianity, the doctrine of self-denial can best be illustrated from the Canonical Books of the Old and New Testament.

* * *

In Genesis, the Fall of man is attributed to disobedience to the will of God, who commanded him not to eat of the tree of the knowledge of good and evil. This tree represents the ego-centric attitude of the unawakened mind, constantly moved by desire and aversion. The result of this attitude is a disproportionate self-consciousness which is nothing less than self-delusion: 'And the eyes of both of them were opened, and they knew that they were naked.' *Genesis* iii.7.

When man is perpetually moved by desire and aversion, greed and hatred, there must come, sooner or later, a growing conviction of the impossibility of ever getting his desire. The unavailing struggle to secure a changeless and constant self-satisfaction induces a corresponding despair, and the final outcome of self-delusion is expulsion from the Garden of Eden to live a life of unrewarding toil.

'Unto the woman he said, I will greatly multiply thy sorrow and conception: in sorrow thou shalt bring forth children: and thy desire shall be to thy husband, and he shall rule over thee.' *Genesis* iii.16.

The woman stands for the subconscious mind or soul which accepts without question the verdicts of the conscious mind. When that mind is in a state of self-delusion, judging all experience from the standpoint of subjective good and evil, the creations of the subconscious mind will always be frustration and disappointment.

'And unto Adam he said, Because thou hast hearkened unto the voice of thy wife, and hast eaten of the tree, of which I commanded thee, saying, Thou shalt not eat of it: cursed is the ground for thy sake; in sorrow shalt thou eat of it all the days of thy life.' *Genesis* iii.17.

'The voice of thy wife' is the reaction of sensation, feeling and emotion, which is the source of the ego-delusion.

This delusion separates man from the Universal Life, and his attitude of self-assertion drives him forth from the Garden of

Eden, that state of perpetual harmony and joy which is the inheritance of the meek.

*   *   *

The story of Cain and Abel, the children of Adam and Eve, is an allegory depicting two opposing and conflicting states of consciousness. The name 'Cain' means possession, and the name 'Abel' means breath.

Cain was a tiller of the ground, and stands for the egocentric attitude of desire and aversion. Consciousness remains fixed in one area, that of a would-be permanent, unchanging self or personality, constantly striving to force the material, external world into conformity with personal desire. This state of consciousness is one of greed and hatred.

Abel, as his name suggests, stands for a higher state of consciousness. Breath is life. While Cain represents the atrophy of consciousness through stagnation in self-delusion, Abel, the keeper of sheep, represents movement and growth. The nomad shepherd moves from one place to another, seeking fresh pasture for his sheep. So the awakened mind seeks fresh aspects of truth, a deeper and more satisfying interpretation of experience.

This growth and movement of consciousness finds its most persistent adversary in the ego-delusion itself: 'And Cain talked with Abel his brother, and it came to pass, when they were in the field, that Cain rose up against Abel his brother, and slew him.' *Genesis* iv.8.

Long-standing and inherited habits of thought, of thinking in terms of 'I' and 'Mine', and the whole attitude of self-assertion, continually rise up to obstruct man's progress in the direction of self-denial and of impersonality. The will to preserve individuality and separation finds its perfect expression in Cain's reply to the Lord: 'And the Lord said unto Cain, Where is Abel thy brother? And he said, I know not. *Am I my brother's keeper?' Genesis* iv.9.

This has always been the response of the self-centred to the claims and obligations of compassion.

Obstinate self-delusion brings its own penalty: 'When thou tillest the ground, it shall not henceforth yield thee her strength; a fugitive and a vagabond shalt thou be in the earth.' *Genesis* iv.12.

The attitude of greed and hatred, of desire and aversion, the demands of an unchanging ego upon a continually changing world can never be satisfied. To defy the laws of life, and to cherish a distorted view of reality, make man an outcast. He separates himself entirely and completely from his fellows, and finally convinces himself that all are against him: 'and it shall come to pass, that every one that findeth me shall slay me'. *Genesis* iv.14.

Self-delusion alienates the mind from the Universal Life, and keeps man always in a state of insecurity and fear: he cannot know the harmony and joy of the enlightened. He remains forever outside the Garden of Eden, 'And Cain went out from the presence of the Lord, and dwelt in the land of Nod, on the east of Eden.' *Genesis* iv.16.

Nod means 'vagabond'.

*   *   *

The story of Noah and the Ark illustrates perfectly the statement that the meek shall inherit the earth.

The wickedness of the world was very great, and this wickedness proceeded from man's imagination, or from the delusions that dominated his mind. 'And God saw that the wickedness of man was great in the earth, and that every imagination of the thoughts of his heart was only evil continually.' *Genesis* vi.5.

35

The illusion of self-hood, inducing greed and hatred, results finally in violence and destruction. 'The earth also was corrupt before God; and the earth was filled with violence.' *Genesis* vi.11.

The Flood represents the wholesale destruction of humanity that is always the logical and inevitable outcome of uncontrolled self-assertion. Only the humble and meek are spared, because they go into the Ark, which is the Presence of God.

The name 'Noah' means repose, rest, consolation, the reward of those who renounce the conflicts of self-assertion. When the waters of the flood have gone down, when the violent have destroyed each other, Noah and his sons, walking with God, co-operating with the Universal Mind, come forth to inherit the earth. 'And God blessed Noah and his sons, and said unto them, Be fruitful, and multiply, and replenish the earth.' *Genesis* ix.1.

6

The Spiritual Journey

THE Old Testament teaches that man moves from the delusion of self-assertion to the humility of enlightenment by coming into contact with the Universal Mind or God.

'Now the Lord had said unto Abram, Get thee out of thy country, and from thy kindred, and from thy father's house, unto a land that I will shew thee.' *Genesis* xii.1.

The land from which Abram departed when he was seventy and five years old was called Haran, the meaning of which is 'mountainous country'. He and his family came into the land of Canaan, which means 'that humbles and subdues'.

The extent to which a man is able to receive and accept the guidance of the Universal Mind is the measure of his spiritual development, and his faith in God brings him out of the darkness of self-delusion.

'And he said unto him, I am the Lord that brought thee out of the Ur of the Chaldees, to give thee this land to inherit it.' *Genesis* xv.7. The Ur of the Chaldees, where Abram was born, means 'the valley of the robbers', or 'the valley of demons'.

Spiritual development is represented as the movement of man from one country to another. Canaan, a land flowing with milk and honey, stands for a state of consciousness which is the inheritance of those who obey the voice of God.

This process of development, however, is not one of smooth and steady growth. The vision of Truth fades away, and there are frequent lapses into the former state of material consciousness.

'And the Lord appeared unto Abram, and said, Unto thy seed will I give this land: and there builded he an altar unto the Lord, who appeared unto him.' *Genesis* xii.7.

This is the moment of vision, but it is difficult to remain for long in this high state of spiritual consciousness. Following a period of fasting from material thought, there comes a sense of emptiness, a feeling of exhaustion, which is described as 'a famine in the land'. *Genesis* xii.10.

Loss of faith results in a return to the realm of physical sensations and emotions, to the state of self-delusion, when the ego or self reasserts its power over the mind. This lapse is represented as 'going down into Egypt'.

Accompanying the return to self-delusion, there is a determined effort to deny the new state of consciousness formed in the moment of vision. 'And it came to pass, when he was come near to enter into Egypt, that he said unto Sarai his wife, Behold now, I know that thou art a fair woman to look upon: Therefore, it shall come to pass, when the Egyptians shall see thee, that they shall say, This is his wife: and they will kill me, but they will save thee alive. Say, I pray thee, thou art my sister, that it may be well with me for thy sake; and my soul shall live because of thee.' *Genesis* xii.11, 12, 13.

Abram was seventy and five years old when he departed out of Haran, and according to *Genesis* xvii.17, Sarai his wife was ten years younger. So when they went down into Egypt, Sarai was at least sixty-five years old, and hardly likely to dazzle the Egyptians with her beauty.

This allegorical portrayal of the result of loss of faith in one's deepest convictions is employed in exactly similar terms several times in Genesis. When Abram sojourned in Gerar, he led Abimelech to believe that Sarai was his sister. When Abimelech the king was warned by God in a dream of the deception,

Abram excused himself by saying: 'And Abraham said, Because I thought, Surely the fear of God is not in this place; and they will slay me for my wife's sake.' *Genesis* xx.11.

Sarah was over ninety years old at this time, so it is obvious the story is not to be taken literally.

Pharaoh, in the first story, like Abimelech in the second, stands for the old self, or ego, built up on physical sensations, feelings and emotions, while Sarai or Sarah, the wife, stands for the soul awakening out of self-delusion.

The same method of portraying this inner conflict between the old and new states of consciousness is used in the story of Isaac. There was a famine in the land, and Isaac went to Abimelech king of the Philistines, unto Gerar. He, too, denies his wife, and declares that Rebekah is his sister.

There is one variation here: God warns Isaac not to go down into Egypt. 'And the Lord appeared unto him, and said, Go not down into Egypt: dwell in the land which I shall tell thee of.' *Genesis* xxvi.2.

The denial of the awakening state of consciousness causes disease: 'And the Lord plagued Pharaoh and his house with great plagues because of Sarai Abram's wife.' *Genesis* xii.17. 'So Abraham prayed unto God: and God healed Abimelech, and his wife, and his maid-servants; and they bare children. For the Lord had fast closed up all the wombs of the house of Abimelech, because of Sarah Abraham's wife.' *Genesis* xx.17.

None the less, there is something to be gained from every experience, and Abram came out of his conflict considerably enriched in spiritual knowledge. 'And Abram went up out of Egypt . . . and was very rich in cattle, in silver and in gold. And he went on his journeys from the south, even to Bethel, unto the place where his tent had been at the beginning, between Bethel and Hai; unto the place of the altar, which he had made there at the first: and there Abram called on the name of the Lord.' *Genesis* xiii.1, 2, 3, 4.

Once the mind is awakened out of self-delusion, in spite of many lapses, the process of enlightenment continues. Abram returns to the state of spiritual consciousness he had attained before physical exhaustion drove him back into sense consciousness, 'down to Egypt'. That he is in a state of growth and development is indicated by the fact that he lives in a tent, which can be moved from one spot to another. The names Bethel and Hai also tell us that his development is incomplete: Bethel means 'house of God', and Hai or Ai means 'a heap of ruins or of rubbish'. Abram pitched his tent between the two.

* * *

The growth of consciousness is pictured as a journey, in which the mind is drawn by strongly opposing forces to dwell for a time in different countries or states of thought. Conflicting attitudes or interpretations of life co-exist in consciousness, but sooner or later a guiding or overruling principle pushes one or other into the background.

Lot, who is variously described as Abram's brother's son and as Abram's brother, stands for the natural man, for the carnal mind of Abram. The ascendancy of the spiritual man is strongly opposed by the natural man. 'And Lot also, which went with Abram, had flocks and herds and tents. And the land was not able to bear them, that they might dwell together: for their substance was great, so that they could not dwell together. And there was a strife between the herdmen of Abram's cattle and the herdmen of Lot's cattle.' *Genesis* xiii.5, 6, 7.

At Abram's suggestion, he and Lot agree to separate, and to go their different ways, 'Abram dwelt in the land of Canaan,

nd Lot dwelt in the cities of the plain, and pitched his tent
oward Sodom.' *Genesis* xiii.12.

This separation refers to that period of human development
when consciousness was divided into two regions: the conscious
and the subconscious. The name Lot means 'hidden', 'wrapt
up', or 'covered'. 'For him (i.e. the primitive man), religion is a
question of life: namely, how to resist and to maintain himself
against the unknown powers which surround him, and how to
attain security and happiness. These unknown powers are not
only the forces of nature but the enigmatic character of even the
simplest things and the uncontrolled psychic forces within himself. These forces which in the course of time have been pushed
down below the threshold of our so-called normal consciousness
by the intellect and which have been artificially confined to the
subconscious regions, were formerly an important part of the
human world. They not only entered the day-consciousness of
man but were projected into the visible world around him,
while the material objects were accepted as parts of the psychic
world.

'In a state of consciousness which puts the projections of our
mind and feelings on the same plane as material objects and
which experiences both as a reality of equal value and similar
laws, in such a state the limit between subjective experience and
objective things is not yet established. Whatever exists is animated and takes part in the life of the experiencing subject to
which it is related in manifold ways as soon as it enters the field
of cognition. Each contact has its reactions on both sides, thus
establishing new relations.

'Therefore from the standpoint of self-preservation it is
necessary to define, to limit, to direct those relations, and to
prevent the tide of phenomena from overpowering and suffocat-
ing the awakening human soul which is still open to all im-

41

pressions like a child and almost as unprotected.' Lama Anagarika Govinda: *The Psychological Attitude of Early Buddhist Philosophy*. (Rider & Co., London.)

The separation of Abram and Lot is an allegorical personification of this process of definition, limitation and direction. To the awakening conscious mind, represented by Abram, the forces represented by Lot were potentially evil. 'But the men of Sodom were wicked, and sinners before the Lord exceedingly.' *Genesis* xiii.13.

So Abram tried to solve his difficulties by dividing his consciousness into two separate compartments: 'Then Abram removed his tent, and dwelt in the plain of Mamre, which is in Hebron, and built there an altar unto the Lord.' *Genesis* xiii.18.

The removal of Abram's tent signifies a new development of consciousness; 'Mamre' means strength and 'Hebron' means society or friendship. At this stage man attempts to dissociate himself from what he regards as his lower nature by resolutely removing his attention from it, and by keeping his eyes fixed upon his vision of God, or his current interpretation of absolute Good. Thus for a time he may reduce the conflict between the flesh and the spirit, and gain strength and harmony within himself by being true to his convictions.

But Abram's tent also signifies that this state of development is but temporary, and that he was only resting before setting forth once more on the long journey to spiritual wholeness.

As long as a man condemns any part of his own nature he condemns himself: the relegation of certain forces into the subliminal or subconscious depths as unworthy or impure will not set him free from the destructive influence of delusion. Nothing less than a true interpretation of Life as Divine and Sacred in its every aspect will suffice to drive out his false concepts of good and evil. Then he will know that all Power is of

God, and that evil exists only in the imaginations of the heart.

That Abram, or Abraham as he was then called, attained to this state of wholeness, is revealed by his readiness, at a later period in his history, to offer his only son Isaac as a burnt-offering to God at Jehovah-jireh: which means that he had reached the depth of spiritual insight by which he was able to relinquish every vestige of the illusion of selfhood.

7

The Decalogue

THE degree of self-denial to be obtained by the enforcement of law is the utmost that can be hoped for as long as men remain in the condition of self-delusion, and the divine origin claimed for the Mosaic Law shows that every advance in human understanding is the result of spiritual vision, when the mind of man establishes contact with the Universal Mind.

'In the third month, when the children of Israel were gone forth out of the land of Egypt, the same day came they into the wilderness of Sinai.' *Exodus* xix.1.

Egypt stands for ignorance and the darkness of worldly delusion. Moses had been called by God to lead the children of Israel out of the bondage which is always the lot of the worldly into a new state of consciousness called the 'land of Canaan', 'and to bring them up out of that land unto a good land and a large, and unto a land flowing with milk and honey'. *Exodus* iii.8.

Canaan is the state of spiritual enlightenment and illumination, and until it is reached, the people are in the wilderness of doubt and confusion. If they are to make any progress at all from anarchy, they must be provided with a code of laws and statutes to regulate their behaviour, and to secure a minimum of self-denial, and such laws and statutes, to command general acceptance, must be regarded as being of superhuman authority.

'And the Lord said unto Moses, Lo, I will come unto thee in a thick cloud, that the people may hear when I speak with thee, and believe thee for ever.' *Exodus* xix.9.

It was on the top of Mount Sinai that Moses received the

Decalogue, or the Ten Words, containing the general principles of the Israelites' duties towards God and his neighbour. 'And he gave unto Moses, when he had made an end of communing with him upon Mount Sinai, two tables of testimony, tables of stone, written with the finger of God.' *Exodus* xxxi.18.

In addition to the Decalogue, Moses is said to have received the book of the covenant, containing the most precise and detailed regulations to govern the people's behaviour in every aspect of family and communal life.

Obedience to law is the result of two forms of self-denial: the acceptance of the existence and of the paramount authority of God, and the acceptance of the rights of others. Such obedience, however, is rare, and the law has to be enforced by penalties. So that its observance is a matter of self-preservation rather than of self-denial. None the less, the very existence of a law proclaiming the supreme authority of God, and setting forth the rights of others, invades the consciousness of the most undeveloped minds, and to that extent reduces the area of self-assertion.

The journey from the darkness and bondage of delusion is long and hard, and not all who set out shall achieve illumination. Even Moses fell short of what was required, and was not allowed to enter the land of Canaan: 'And the Lord spake unto Moses that self-same day, saying, Get thee up into this mountain Abarim, unto Mount Nebo, which is in the land of Moab, that is over against Jericho, and behold the land of Canaan, which I give unto the children of Israel for a possession. And die in the mount whither thou goest up, and be gathered unto thy people, as Aaron thy brother died in mount Hor, and was gathered unto his people: because ye trespassed against me among the children of Israel at the waters of Meribah-kadesh, in the wilderness of Zin: because ye sanctified me not in the midst of the children of Israel. Yet thou shalt see the land before thee; but thou shalt not go thither unto the land which I give the children of Israel.' *Deuteronomy* xxii.48-52.

Wilful disobedience is self-assertion; the delusion of selfhood separates the soul from the Universal Soul, and, therefore, no matter how much advance has been made in spiritual knowledge, the soul remains in the wilderness, and cannot enter the realm of perfect illumination. Moses had disobeyed the Lord by striking the rock twice with his rod instead of speaking to it as he had been instructed. 'And the Lord spake unto Moses and Aaron, Because ye believed me not, to sanctify me in the eyes of the children of Israel, therefore ye shall not bring this congregation into the land which I have given them.' *Numbers* xx.12.

None of the men who went out of Egypt ever saw the land of Canaan, for they died in the wilderness, 'because they obeyed not the voice of the Lord'. *Joshua* v.6.

*   *   *

The first commandment in the Decalogue is: 'Thou shalt have no other gods before me.'

Primitive man worshipped many gods, who represented the forces of Nature, in order to propitiate and control them for his own purposes. There was no question of morality or ethics: he was concerned only with his bodily existence, with his own well-being. And this concern was necessary for his preservation. At this stage of his development, primitive man had the innocent preoccupation of a child with his own needs, and as he was as yet hardly self-conscious, there could be no question of self-denial.

As man began to recognize the relationship between the various natural forces the number of his gods was gradually reduced, and more power was ascribed to some gods than to others, and in the course of time this process of simplification reached its logical conclusion in monotheism. There is in Deuteronomy a clear statement of this belief: 'Know therefore this day, and consider it in thine heart, that the Lord he is God in heaven above and upon the earth beneath; there is none else.' *Deuteronomy* iv.39.

The development of the human mind, however unequal in any given period, is, at its highest point, the result of the pressure of circumstance, and new attitudes to life are formed to meet the demands of self-preservation. Self-assertion is continually modified in accordance with it, and to the prophet, to whom God, representing the sum total of all the forces and powers of Nature, was as real as anything in the visible world, it was no flight of fancy to claim for fresh concepts of justice and right behaviour the authority of divine inspiration.

The second commandment, prohibiting idolatry, was necessary to strengthen the first commandment, and to confirm the sanctity of the law.

The third and fourth commandments had the same purpose: to uphold the majesty and authority of God. Reverence for the Divine Name, and the observance of the seventh day by cessation from all labour, as the sabbath of the Lord God, provided practical means to assist in the cultivation of a religious attitude.

Respect for Law is most likely to be found among those who have been trained to respect the authority of their parents: The fifth commandment, 'Honour thy father and thy mother', sought to strengthen still further the hold of external authority, and to confine within well-defined limits the natural waywardness of man.

The first five commandments, that is to say, one half of the Decalogue, are thus concerned with imposing the strongest possible external restraints upon the ego, the self, the human personality: an indication of a profound awareness of the intractable power of self-delusion.

That this delusion expresses itself invariably as desire and aversion, greed and hatred, is clearly and explicitly stated in the remaining five commandments.

'Thou shalt not kill.' Of all the acts of hatred of which man, in the darkness of self-delusion, is capable, murder is the most complete and final. Hatred of all obstacles to the satisfaction of desire is the negative aspect of the twofold symptom of delusion. The positive aspect of this symptom, desire in its most uncontrolled expression, is dealt with in the seventh commandment: 'Thou shalt not commit adultery.'

The eighth commandment is designed to keep greed within bounds: 'Thou shalt not steal'; and the ninth: 'Thou shalt not bear false witness against thy neighbour', to bridle the lying mouth of hatred.

And last of all, the tenth commandment deals with the source of all cruelty: 'Thou shalt not covet thy neighbour's house, thou shalt not covet thy neighbour's wife, nor his man-servant, nor his maid-servant, nor his ox, nor his ass, nor any thing that is thy neighbour's.' *Exodus* xx.17.

The Mosaic Law makes no attempt to expose or condemn self-delusion, it merely seeks to prevent those expressions of desire and aversion, of greed and hatred, most likely to injure others, and which, if not regulated by a central authority, would lead to anarchy.

The ego-delusion, which leads to every crime, makes necessary the establishment of law, and the very existence of law is sufficient proof of the almost complete ignorance in which humanity strives with tragic obstinacy to secure a happiness as insubstantial and unreal as a desert mirage.

8

The God of Moses

THE establishment of Law marks a major advance in the history of human thought, and is the first signpost on the journey from the anarchy and bondage of absolute selfhood to the freedom of self-denial. Since the Mosaic Law is described as the utterance of God, it is necessary to understand the Mosaic conception of God.

Moses's first contact with God is described in the account of the burning bush. 'And the angel of the Lord appeared unto him in a flame of fire out of the midst of a bush: and he looked, and behold the bush burned with fire, and the bush was not consumed.' *Exodus* iii.2. A flame of fire gives light and heat, and stands for the invisible force of life itself. The bush which was not consumed represents the outward visible forms animated and sustained by the life force.

God called to Moses out of the midst of the bush: 'Draw not nigh hither: put off thy shoes from off thy feet; for the place whereon thou standest is holy ground. Moreover he said, I am the God of thy father, the God of Abraham, the God of Isaac, and the God of Jacob. And Moses hid his face; for he was afraid to look upon God'. *Exodus* iii.5, 6.

The God of Moses is thus revealed as the omnipresent Spirit, the Universal Life manifesting itself in innumerable visible forms. God is everywhere, and everywhere is holy ground. When man reaches a high state of spiritual consciousness, he is able to hear the voice of God.

The God who speaks with Moses is a God of compassion,

who sees the affliction of His people: 'for I know their sorrow.' Moreover, He is a God whose compassion moves Him to action. He calls Moses to go to Pharaoh, that he may bring forth the children of Israel out of Egypt.

Having called Moses to perform this task, He will not listen to any of his arguments. He reasons with him and finally persuades him to do His will. Since the bondage and afflictions of the children of Israel represent the sufferings of humanity in the darkness of worldly delusion, it is clearly the will of God that mankind should be led out of this darkness, and for this purpose He calls men of high spiritual consciousness to be leaders and prophets and teachers. And to some God grants certain miraculous powers, that they may be able to do what is required of them. To the reluctant and the fearful, He promises the assurance of His abiding Presence at all times: 'And he said, Certainly I will be with thee.' *Exodus* iii.12.

The God of Moses is the Supreme Cause of all effects: 'And the Lord said unto him. Who hath made man's mouth? or who maketh the dumb, or deaf, or the seeing, or the blind? Have not I the Lord?' *Exodus* iv.11.

The struggle between Moses and Pharaoh is the struggle between the superconscious and the subconscious minds of man. Spiritual intimations and urgings to seek a higher source of good are received by the superconscious mind, while the subconscious mind, conditioned by race inheritance and worldly beliefs, clings stubbornly to its familiar delusions. The children of Israel stand for all the innumerable thoughts and impulses in the subconscious mind. It is these that must be set free from their subjection to self-delusion.

The account of Moses's dealings with Pharaoh, gives, in an allegorical form, a striking illustration of the reactions of a deeply conditioned subconscious mind to the suggestions of an unconvinced and wavering conscious mind. Moses had little faith in his ability to persuade Pharaoh to let the people go, that they might sacrifice to the Lord their God in the wilderness. 'And Moses said unto the Lord, O, my Lord, I am not eloquent, neither heretofore, nor since thou hast spoken unto thy servant.' *Exodus* iv.10. 'And Moses spake before the Lord, saying, Behold, the children of Israel have not hearkened unto me; how then shall Pharaoh hear me, who am of uncircumcised lips?' *Exodus* vi.12.

Pharaoh refuses to listen to Moses and Aaron, and declares that he does not know the Lord. He increases the bondage of the Israelites by forcing them to make bricks without straw. They had to go and gather stubble, because they were refused straw, and were expected to make as many bricks as before. This shows how the subconscious mind, conditioned by the ego-delusion, stubbornly resists any attempt to bring it into new ways of thinking, and continues to waste the life force in futile occupations which can give no lasting benefits.

This unwillingness on the part of the subconscious mind to adopt a new attitude is described as 'hardening the heart'. 'And I will harden Pharaoh's heart . . .' *Exodus* vii.3.

The heart in ancient allegories always stands for the subconscious mind. The struggle to change the attitude of the heart is a hard one, for it will not be convinced by miracles, or by plagues, or by natural calamities. Only one thing will set the life energies free to worship God: the death of the ego-delusion. 'And it came to pass that at midnight the Lord smote all the first-born in the land of Egypt, from the first-born of Pharaoh that sat on his throne unto the first-born of the captive that was in the dungeon; and all the first-born of cattle.' *Exodus* xii.29.

The first-born is a term which has the same meaning as 'thine only son', or the 'only begotten son', and represents the ego or limited personality of man, or the fulness of the personality of God. Abraham was called upon to offer his only son, Isaac, as a sacrifice to God. Jesus Christ is described as the only begotten Son: 'No man hath seen God at any time: the only begotten Son, which is in the bosom of the Father, he hath declared him.' *John* 1.18.

The passage of the Israelites from Egypt through the Red Sea, led by God, by day in a pillar of a cloud and by night in a pillar of fire, represents the movement of the mind from a lower to a higher state of consciousness. This cannot take place without geting rid of old long-established ideas: 'and the Lord overthrew the Egyptians in the midst of the sea.' *Exodus* xiv.27.

*   *   *

The God of Moses was exclusively the God of the children of Israel, and they were His people whom He had redeemed. It was to Him that they turned to supply their need of water and food. In return, they were to obey His commandments. 'If thou wilt diligently hearken to the voice of the Lord thy God, and wilt do that which is right in his sight, and wilt give ear to his commandments, and keep all his statutes, I will put none of these diseases upon thee, which I have brought upon the Egyptians: for I am the Lord that healeth thee.' *Exodus* xv.26.

Full co-operation with the Universal Life cannot be achieved without complete self-denial, the rejection of the self-delusion which is the source of all human suffering.

The relationship between God and Moses is described as a personal intimacy: 'And the Lord spake unto Moses face to face, as a man speaketh unto his friend.' *Exodus* xxxiii.11. Human emotions are ascribed to God, such as impatience and anger, and the desire to destroy those who oppose His will. Like a man,

He can be persuaded to change His mind. 'Turn from thy fierce wrath, and repent of this evil against thy people . . . And the Lord repented of the evil which he had thought to do unto his people.' *Exodus* xxxii.12, 14.

The difficulties which Moses had with the people show how great is the struggle to control natural instincts and to get rid of firmly established habits of thought. All idolatrous tendencies must be eliminated, as Moses slew three thousand men who had worshipped the golden calf. It is also made clear that the consequences of sinful deeds cannot be avoided. 'Therefore now go, lead the people unto the place of which I have spoken unto thee: behold, mine Angel shall go before thee; nevertheless, in the day when I visit, I will visit their sin upon them.' *Exodus* xxxii.34.

The God of Moses withdraws Himself from those who will not obey His voice: His Presence is vouchsafed only to those who earnestly seek it. 'And he said. My presence shall go with thee, and I will give thee rest.' *Exodus* xxxiii.14.

The intimate relationship between God and Moses is permitted only to those of the highest spiritual development, and any anthropomorphic impressions are corrected by another aspect of God portrayed in Exodus, in which He appears as unutterably awesome and immeasureably superior to man. Only Moses and Aaron were to go up Mount Sinai to hear the law: but the priests and the people were forbidden on pain of death even to touch the border of the mount. 'And the Lord said unto him, get thee down, and thou shalt come up, thou, and Aaron with thee: but let not the priests and the people break through to come up unto the Lord, lest he break forth upon them.' *Exodus* xix.24.

A power of unimaginable force proceeds from the Presence of God, and only those who have by long practice trained the physical organism to receive its vibrations can survive contact with it. 'And the sight of the glory of God was like a devouring fire, on the top of the mount, in the eyes of the children of Israel.' *Exodus* xxv.17.

Even Moses could not stand the full force of this power: 'And he said, Thou canst not see my face: for there shall no man see me, and live.' *Exodus* xxxiii.20.

Moses stayed on the mount for forty days and forty nights, which means that he was in a high state of spiritual consciousness for a long period, during which he fasted: 'he did neither eat bread, nor drink water.' At the outset of His ministry, Jesus Christ spent a similar period in fasting and meditation.

This prolonged communion with the Universal Soul or God had produced a marked change in Moses: his face shone from an inner radiance: 'And when Aaron and all the children of Israel saw Moses, behold, the skin of his face shone, and they were afraid to come nigh him ... And till Moses had done speaking with them he put a vail on his face.' *Exodus* xxxiv.33.

The shedding of the veils of self-delusion allows the Spirit within to reveal itself as pure light. Moses is an outstanding example of this high state of spiritual development. 'Now the man Moses was very meek, above all the men which were upon the face of the earth.' *Numbers* xii.3.

Unlike lesser leaders of men, he was entirely free from jealousy. When the Lord gave a portion of the spirit that was upon Moses to the seventy elders that they might be able to help him, there was some resentment among the people: 'And there ran a young man, and told Moses, and said, Eldad and Medad do prophesy in the camp. And Joshua the son of Nun, the servant of Moses, one of his young men, answered and said, My lord Moses, forbid them. And Moses said unto him, Enviest thou for my sake? Would God that all the Lord's people were

prophets, and that the Lord would put his Spirit upon them.'
Numbers xi.27, 28, 29.

Moses had freed himself from self-delusion to such an extent
that he saw himself as the instrument of God: 'And Moses said,
Hereby ye shall know that the Lord hath sent me to do all these
works: for I have not done them of my own mind.' *Numbers*
xvi.28.

Self-denial is thus revealed as the consecration of the life-
force to the service of God. The lusts of the flesh are compared
to fiery serpents, which bit the people of Israel, so that many of
them died. They stand for the uncontrolled activities of the life
force. The Lord revealed to Moses what has to be done: 'And
the Lord said unto Moses, Make thee a fiery serpent, and set it
upon a pole; and it shall come to pass, that every one that is
bitten, when he looketh upon it, shall live. And Moses made a
serpent of brass, and put it upon a pole; and it came to pass,
that if a serpent had bitten any man, when he beheld the serpent
of brass, he lived.' *Numbers* xxi.8, 9.

The meaning of this allegory is made clear by the words of
Jesus Christ as recorded in the Gospel according to St John:
'And as Moses lifted up the serpent in the wilderness, even so
must the Son of man be lifted up: that whosoever believeth in
him should not perish, but have eternal life.' *John* iii.14, 15.

To make a serpent of brass was to objectify the invisible life-
force, and thereby obtain mastery over it. The primitive man
believed that the name of an object, or an image of it, were em-
bodiments of its power, and by giving it a name or by making
an image of it, that power could be controlled.

Self-denial is the process of controlling and mastering the
energies of the life-force, and of raising them from the lowest
centres of consciousness to the highest.

In the Hindu Scriptures the life-force or spiritual energy is called the 'Kundalini', which means 'the Serpent Power'. It is the spiritual energy lying dormant in all individuals, a huge reserve of force lying coiled up at the base of the spine. The purpose of the Indian method of meditation called raja yoga is to arouse the kundalini, and to cause it to ascend through the various centres of consciousness situated in the spinal column until it reaches the seventh centre in the top of the head. This is the highest goal, and here the awakened spiritual energy reaches its highest state of consciousness.

The same ideas are an important part of Buddhist meditation 'The susumna (i.e. the hollow canal which runs through the centre of the spinal cord) is closed at its lower end, as long as the latent creative forces of the Kundalini are not awakened. In this state the Kundalini, which is likened to a coiled serpent (the symbol of latent energy), blocks the entrance to the susumna. By awakening the Kundalini's dormant forces, which otherwise are absorbed in subconscious and purely bodily functions, and by directing them to the higher centres, the energies thus released are transformed and sublimated until their perfect unfoldment and conscious realization is achieved in the highest centre.' Lama Anagarica Govinda: *Foundations of Tibetan Mysticism*. (Rider & Company, London.)

The pole on which Moses set the brass serpent may well have been a crude representation of the spinal column: the life energies occupied with sense appetites must be raised from the earth in which the bottom of the pole is stuck, to animate and invigorate the highest spiritual centre in the brain. Thus only can man achieve the enlightenment and liberation of self-denial.

9

The God of Job

THE search for the purpose and meaning of life which is under-
taken by the awakened mind of man shaking himself free from
self-delusion leads to the acceptance of a belief in a Universal
Mind, in the existence of God. But when this stage is reached,
new difficulties arise, because the finite human mind is unable
to comprehend the infinite mind of God.

The God of Moses presented no difficulties to the human
mind: He was just and merciful. He entered into the lives of the
people of Israel under certain well-defined conditions. He made
a covenant or a bargain with them. In return for obedience to
His commandments, He promised them protection, long life
and prosperity. Failure to keep this bargain meant adversity
and death. It was all very simple and clear-cut. 'Know therefore that the Lord thy God, he is God, the faithful God, which
keepeth covenant and mercy with them that love him, and keep
his commandments, to a thousand generations; and repayeth
them that hate him to their face, to destroy them: he will not
be slack to him that hateth him, he will repay him to his face.'
Deuteronomy vii.9, 10.

'See, I have set before thee this day life and good, and death
and evil. In that I command thee this day to love the Lord thy
God, and to walk in his ways, and to keep his commandments,
and his statutes, and his judgements, that thou mayest live and
multiply: and the Lord thy God shall bless thee in the land
whither thou goest to possess it. But if thine heart turn away,
so that thou wilt not hear, but shalt be drawn away, and worship

57

other gods and serve them; I denounce unto you this day that
ye shall surely perish, and that ye shall not prolong your days
upon the land whither thou passest over Jordan to go to possess
it.' *Deuteronomy* xxx.15, 16, 17, 18.

This doctrine of rewards for the righteous and retribution for
the wicked, so logical and satisfying to the human mind, was
difficult to maintain in the face of the hard facts of experience.
The prophet Habakkuk, writing about 560-500 B.C., said: 'O
Lord, how long shall I cry and thou wilt not hear? even cry out
unto thee of violence, and thou wilt not save?... Thou art of
purer eyes than to behold evil, and canst not look on iniquity:
wherefore lookest thou upon them that deal treacherously, and
holdest thy tongue when the wicked devoureth the man that is
more righteous than he?' *Habakkuk* i.2, 13.

At the end of the fifth century or the beginning of the fourth
century B.C., the prophet Jeremiah was asking: 'Righteous art
thou, O Lord, when I plead with thee; yet let me talk with thee
of thy judgements. Wherefore doth the way of the wicked prosper? wherefore are all they happy that deal very treacherously?'
Jeremiah xii.1.

In the seventy-third Psalm, written between 500 and 300
B.C., we read: 'For I was envious at the foolish, when I saw the
prosperity of the wicked... Behold, these are the ungodly,
who prosper in the world; they increase in riches.' *Psalm* 73.3-
12.

The Book of Job, which was written between the middle of
the fifth and the middle of the fourth century B.C., was an
attempt to discuss the problem of the righteousness of God in
the face of the prosperity of the wicked and the afflictions of the
innocent.

The case is very clearly presented: 'There was a man in the
land of Uz, whose name was Job; and that man was perfect and

upright, and one that feared God and eschewed evil.' *Job* i.1.

Job was a wealthy and prosperous man: 'so that this man was the greatest of all the men of the east.' He had seven sons and three daughters, and was, in all, a perfect illustration of the doctrine of rewards and punishments.

The author of the Book of Job had thought very deeply about this doctrine, and not only found it difficult to reconcile with the facts of human experience, but also questioned the sincerity of the worship of God inspired by it. Was it anything more than self-seeking? When the Lord praised his servant Job as a perfect and an upright man, Satan answered: 'Doth Job fear God for nought? Hast not thou made an hedge about him, and about his house, and about all that he hath on every side? thou hast blessed the work of his hands, and his substance is increased in the land.' *Job* i.9, 10.

Satan was given permission to test the sincerity of Job by bringing upon him a series of calamities in which he lost his sons and daughters, his servants, and all his sheep, camels and oxen. From the height of his wealth and happiness he was suddenly plunged into the depths of great grief and poverty. But Job's faith in God was not shaken: 'Then Job arose and rent his mantle, and shaved his head, and fell down upon the ground and worshipped, and said: "Naked came I out of my mother's womb, and naked shall I return thither: the Lord gave, and the Lord hath taken away; blessed be the name of the Lord."' *Job* i.20, 21.

When the Lord renewed his praise of Job, Satan argued that the test had not been severe enough: 'But put forth thine hand now, and touch his bone and his flesh, and he will curse thee to thy face.' *Job* ii.5.

So Job was stricken with 'sore boils from the sole of his foot unto his crown'. Yet, in spite of the taunts of his wife, he refused to curse God. 'What! shall we receive good at the hand of God, and shall we not receive evil? In all this did not Job sin with his lips.' *Job* ii.10.

Job's three friends, Eliphaz the Temanite, and Bildad the Shuhite, and Zophar the Naamathite, came to comfort him. They were champions of the orthodox view that adversity and disease were punishments for sin, and tried to convince Job of his guilt. 'Even as I have seen, they that plow iniquity, and sow wickedness, reap the same.' *Job* iv.8.

Eliphaz tried to persuade Job to look upon his calamities as punishment for wrong-doing, and to accept them in a proper spirit of humility. 'Behold, happy is the man whom God correcteth: therefore despise not thou the chastening of the Lord. For he maketh sore, and bindeth up: he woundeth and his hands make whole.' *Job* v.17, 18.

There can be no doubt that, before his calamities came upon him, Job fully accepted the doctrine of rewards and punishments, and had been most scrupulous in the performance of his religious duties. 'And his sons went and feasted in their houses, every one his day; and sent and called for their three sisters to eat and to drink with them. And it was so, when the days of their feasting were gone about, that Job sent and sanctified them, and rose up early in the morning, and offered burnt-offerings according to the number of them all: for Job said, it may be that my sons have sinned, and cursed God in their hearts. Thus did Job continually.' *Job* i.4, 5.

To the annoyance and indignation of his three friends, Job refused to admit his guilt; on the contrary, he insisted that he was being punished without cause. 'O that one would hear me! Behold, my desire is that the Almighty would answer me, and that mine adversary had written a book.' *Job* xxxi.35.

None the less, Job had not lost his faith in God: 'All the while my breath is in me, and the Spirit of God is in my nostrils, my lips shall not speak wickedness, nor my tongue utter deceit. My righteousness I hold fast, and will not let it go: my heart shall not reproach me so long as I live.' *Job* xxvii.3, 4.

Job believed that if the solution to his problem could not be found in this world, then everything would be made plain in the next. 'For I know that my Redeemer liveth, and that he shall stand at the latter day upon the earth, and though after my skin worms destroy this body, yet in my flesh shall I see God, whom I shall see for myself, and mine eyes shall behold, and not another.' *Job* xix.25, 26, 27.

God accepted Job's challenge to answer him, but the reply given contains no direct solution of the sufferings of the innocent. It gives a vivid picture of the majesty and power of God, and charges Job with ignorance. 'Who is this that darkeneth counsel by words without knowledge?' But the answer satisfied Job: he admitted his ignorance and submitted himself to the will of God: 'Who is he that hideth counsel without knowledge? therefore have I uttered that I understood not: things too wonderful for me, which I knew not.' *Job* xlii.3, 4.

Throughout the period of his calamities, Job had been searching for God. The real cause of his intense mental anguish was his self-assertion. But when he found God, his self-assertion vanished, to be replaced by the utter self-denial of true humility. 'I have heard of thee by the hearing of the ear; but now mine eye seeth thee. Wherefore I abhor myself, and repent in dust and ashes.' *Job* xlii.5, 6.

The Book of Job shows a profound understanding of spiritual truth; the three friends of Job were condemned for their false views about God, 'for ye have not spoken of me the thing that is right, as my servant Job hath.' *Job* xlii.7.

The orthodox doctrine of rewards and punishments upheld by

Eliphaz, Bildad, and Zophar, is one of dualism, of separation between God and man, and is the real source of his suffering. When Job achieved self-denial, his troubles came to an end. 'And the Lord turned the captivity of Job when he prayed for his friends: also the Lord gave Job twice as much as he had before.' *Job* xlii.10.

Many commentators have pondered over the solution to the problem of pain and of 'innocent' suffering offered by the Book of Job, and have found it unsatisfactory. 'The striking fact in the poet's discussion is that the divine pronouncement at the end contains no hint at an answer. God simply presents Himself as He is, and Job is cowed, and abhors himself in dust and ashes. This is no solution of the problem, and the poet cannot have intended it to be understood as one. In other words, it looks as though he had deliberately told his readers that there was no solution—at least none that the human mind could appreciate.' Oesterley and Robinson: *An Introduction To The Books of The Old Testament.* (S.P.C.K.)

The author of the Book of Job, like the Buddha, and Jesus, understood very clearly that the cause of all human suffering is the delusion of a separate self or personality. It is the delusion of a self with definite claims and rights that creates a problem which has no reality except in the deluded human mind. A true knowledge and vision of God as He is destroys this delusion, and self-assertion gives place at once to utter self-denial. Self-denial, as understood by the Buddha in his doctrine of Anatta, and by Jesus Christ in the acceptance of the Cross, is the solution offered by the author of the Book of Job. When the self is recognized as a delusion of the purely human mind, then it is seen clearly that there is no self who desires prosperity, there is no self to complain of suffering: there is only God.

Job's calamities were the result of his own ignorance of

spiritual laws, and of his inadequate conception of God. His early worship of God was no more than the normal expression of self-delusion, i.e. desire and aversion. He desired to remain prosperous, he feared destruction. 'For destruction from God was a terror to me, and by reason of his highness I could not endure.' *Job* xxxi.23. He constantly feared what God could do to him, and fear always brings into being the thing that is feared. For the thing which I greatly feared is come upon me, and that which I was afraid of is come unto me.' *Job* iii.25.

The catalogue of God's mighty works which is given at the end of the Book of Job in answer to Job's challenge seems entirely irrelevant to those commentators who miss the point of the answer. But to Job it was the vision of God as He is: the Universal Conscious Life animating all forms, and sustaining the whole Creation. In the Presence of this Infinite Spirit, self-assertion dwindles to nothing, and with the disappearance of the ego-entity, of a selfhood apart from God, there can be no longer any problem of suffering, because desire and aversion will have ceased to exist.

10

The Cross of Self-Denial

It is in the teachings of Jesus Christ that we find the most explicit statement of the paramount necessity for self-denial. 'Then said Jesus unto his disciples, If any man will come after me, let him deny himself, and take up his cross and follow me. For whosoever will save his life shall lose it; and whosoever will lose his life for my sake shall find it.' *Matthew* xvi.24, 25.

The Romans reserved the punishment of death on the cross for slaves, foreigners and desperate criminals, and to them it was the most shameful death. To the Jews, likewise, the death on the cross was regarded with utter abhorrence because, according to their Law, it came under the curse of God, 'for he that is hanged (i.e. on a tree) is accursed of God.' *Deuteronomy* xxi.23. A condemned man was compelled to carry the transverse beam of his own cross to the place of crucifixion, and the disciples must have often witnessed such a scene.

Jesus was, therefore, by using this figure of speech, making His meaning unmistakably clear that by self-denial He meant a slow, lingering form of death similar to that of the cross. In crucifixion the victim stayed alive sometimes for several days, and when at last death came to end his sufferings, it was more from lack of food and exhaustion rather than loss of blood.

Self-denial is the slow and painful process of destroying the delusion of a separate personality or ego. The will to begin and to continue this process is the test of genuine discipleship: 'And he that taketh not his cross, and followeth after me, is not worthy of me.' *Matthew* x.38.

Those who cling to the life of self-delusion will eventually lose it, but those who are willing to renounce that life for the sake of Christ, will discover the true life which cannot be lost. This true life is the Christ, or spiritual consciousness, which, reflecting the Universal Mind, identifies itself with it, 'For it is not ye that speak, but the Spirit of the Father which speaketh in you.' *Matthew* x.20.

Jesus had already identified Himself completely with the Universal Life: 'Jesus said unto them, verily, verily, I say unto you, Before Abraham was, I am.' *John* viii.58. He spoke even more plainly when He said: 'I and my Father are one.' *John* x.30.

He taught His disciples that the Life of which He was the incarnation was eternal, without beginning or ending, and that all who disowned the personal ego, the delusion of a separate self, would enter into His own state of consciousness, and would be aware that they possessed the same eternal life. 'My sheep hear my voice, and I know them, and they follow me: and I give unto them eternal life, and they shall never perish, neither shall any pluck them out of my hand.' *John* x.27, 28.

The sheep of Christ are those who have given up all self-assertion, who are free from desire and aversion, from greed and hatred, and listen only to the inner voice of the Life within. Jesus came to point the way out of delusion: 'I am the door of the sheep.' *John* x.7. Every form of self-delusion He compares to thieves and robbers which take possession of the life energies of man for their own purposes. 'The thief cometh not, but for to steal, and to destroy: I am come that they might have life, and that they might have it more abundantly.' *John* x.10.

The endless succession of desires and aversions based on the delusion of a separate ego or self, which forms the unenlightened state of consciousness, can lead to nothing but disappointment, weariness of spirit and constant frustration, ending finally in bitterness and utter despair. The Christ is the state of consciousness of those who have freed themselves from the burden of the self, and have identified themselves with the Universal Mind and Spirit.

Although self-denial or the renunciation of the concept of a separate personality or ego is likened to the death of the cross, it is only the death of the lowest state of consciousness into which man is born. With the disappearance of self-delusion, there is no loss, but rather an expansion of consciousness. There is a new sense of freedom from the cares which spring from self-concern, an ever increasing contentment, and joy. 'These things have I spoken unto you that my joy might remain in you, and that your joy might be full.' *John* xv.11. 'Hitherto have ye asked nothing in my name: ask, and ye shall receive, that your joy may be full.' *John* xvi.24.

Freedom from self-concern makes available a new source of joy, completely independent of the movement of events in the outer world. The elimination of the delusion of an unchanging ego removes the main obstacle to the spirit of service which is the real expression of the life within. Impersonal love and compassion become the motive of all action, instead of desire and aversion, greed and hatred.

The account of the temptation of Jesus by the devil shows how he refused to descend into the lowest state of consciousness in which the unenlightened man continually dwells. He would not turn stones into bread, i.e. He would not fall into the error of trying to satisfy His soul with material objects. He would not cast himself down from the pinnacle of the temple, i.e. from a high state of spiritual vision, even once; nor would He be seduced into the labyrinth of desire by the offer of the kingdoms of the world and the glory of them.

66

* * *

Behaviour has its source in the attitude of mind, and human behaviour is commonly governed by the illusion of selfhood, which finds its ultimate and most logical expression in the philosophy of self-preservation.

The ideal way to transform human behaviour would be to substitute the truth of self-denial for the delusions of self-assertion, but Jesus knew that the people whom He was trying to teach were not sufficiently developed to be able to understand this truth. Since the attitude of mind could not immediately be destroyed, it was possible only to attempt to deal with the results of that attitude. Self-denial had to be introduced piecemeal into human conduct, so that some of the fruits of enlightenment might be shown before enlightenment itself was achieved.

Thus right conduct becomes the deliberate choice of those who, while still in a state of self-delusion, accept certain limitations of the self under the influence of their teachers. Such a process of self-denial is not without its dangers, and may even strengthen the delusion of a separate self, and lead to self-righteousness. A life lived strictly in accordance with an accepted moral code, involving severe limitations of self-assertion, may still be a life of spiritual blindness. 'For I say unto you, that except your righteousness shall exceed the righteousness of the scribes and Pharisees, ye shall in no case enter into the kingdom of Heaven.' *Matthew* v.20.

Jesus was well aware of the dangers of a selective form of self-denial, and condemned the self-righteousness of the religious leaders of His own day. Yet He felt He had to try to throw the light of truth on questions of behaviour before it was possible for his hearers to grasp the full implications of the doctrine of self-denial.

The type of conduct taught in the Sermon on the Mount was

in itself startling enough, and incomprehensible to the un-enlightened. Even today millions of so-called Christians regard the doctrine of non-resistance to evil as utterly impracticable. 'But I say unto you, That ye resist not evil; but whosoever shall strike thee on thy right cheek, turn to him the other also.' *Matthew* v.39. To the great majority, this teaching is unreason-able and absurd.

The self-denial taught by Jesus is understood as a form of discipline to be applied by each man as, and when, he thinks fit: an example of this attitude is the practice of not smoking or not eating sweets in Lent. But there is no question of under-standing self-denial as the denial of the existence of the self. There is not the faintest glimmer of the Buddhist doctrine of Impersonality: 'Within there is no self that acts, and outside there is no self affected by the action.' Nyanaponika Thera: *The Heart of Buddhist Meditation*. (Rider & Company, London.)

Jesus himself was entirely free from all trace of the delusion of a separate self: 'I can of mine own self do nothing: as I hear, I judge: and my judgment is just; because I seek not mine own will, but the will of the Father which hath sent me. If I bear witness of myself, my witness is not true.' *John* v.30, 31.

He identified the life within Him with the Universal Life which He called the Father: 'I and my Father are one.' *John* x.30.

He proclaimed that the Life has its own will and that He had no will of His own. 'My meat is to do the will of him that sent me, and to finish his work.' *John* iv.34. The task of Jesus was to lead men into the kingdom of God, the state of consciousness which has grown out of the darkness of self-delusion into the light and freedom of self-denial.

The result of entering the kingdom of God is to inherit eternal life, but to cling to any material possession is to remain in the consciousness of change, of corruption and of death. The young man who had great possessions was not willing to sell all that he had, and give it to the poor, and therefore identified himself with what was merely temporal and perishable. 'And Jesus looked round about, and saith unto his disciples, How hardly shall they that have riches enter into the kingdom of God.' *Mark* x.23.

Jesus himself resisted all attempts to ascribe to Him an identity separate from that of the Universal Life. When the young man who had great possessions addressed Him as 'Good Master', Jesus rebuked him, 'Why callest thou me good? there is none good but one, that is, God.' Not only is trust in riches to be regarded as an obstacle to the achievement of self-denial, but all human ties must be abandoned, because they foster the delusion of a separate self or personality. 'And Jesus answered and said, There is no man that hath left house, or brethren, or sisters, or father, or mother, or wife, or children, or lands, for my sake and the gospel's, but he shall receive an hundredfold now in this time, houses, and brethren, and sisters, and mothers, and children, and lands, with persecutions; and in the world to come eternal life.' *Mark* x.29, 30.

The enlightened disciple, with the growth of self-denial, will see himself as a member of the family of God, sustained and inspired by the one Father, the life of every living creature. His wealth is in his own consciousness, aware of the true nature of the life within him, '. . . thou shalt have treasure in heaven; and come, take up the cross, and follow me.' *Mark* x.21.

The young man with great possessions stands for every man who is not willing to renounce the ego-illusion, for when all is said and done, a man's most cherished possession is this illusion. Even when the truth of Impersonality has been grasped, the delusion of personality with ever active desires and aversions is so firmly rooted in consciousness, that only by persistent denial and control of automatic and habitual egocentric reactions to changing events can this delusion be finally destroyed.

I I

The Inner Attitude

N the Sermon on the Mount, Jesus examines behaviour, and condemns hypocrisy. He knew that the Jews, under the domination of the ego-delusion, believed that the outward observance of the Mosaic Law was all that was required of them, and that his attitude fostered insincerity and cynicism; a self-conscious obedience to the commandments merely gave rise to new forms of self-deception and self-assertion.

In the state of delusion, the ego is able to exploit the most unlikely situations for its own purposes, and to turn what was meant to be an act of self-denial into an occasion for self-display. Alms-giving, prayer and fasting became opportunities for ostentation, and were, therefore, spiritually worthless.

Acts of piety performed to impress men were of no value, and long prayers useless. God, being omniscient and omnipresent, knows all a man's needs before he asks. The Lord's Prayer which Jesus gave as an example, is a pattern of brevity and simplicity, and combining reverence with directness, is a perfect expression of the right attitude of mind in which to approach God. Such a prayer must be made in secret, in the privacy of one's own room, 'when thou hast shut thy door', and being therefore a sincere utterance of the soul, cannot fail to be answered.

Jesus reminded his listeners, however, that man cannot be forgiven unless he himself forgives. Without forgiveness, there is separation, and to separate oneself even from one man, is to separate oneself from God.

71

In His discussion of the Commandments, Jesus went behind the outward action to the inner motive. It is not enough to refrain from heinous deeds, it is necessary to eradicate their cause, because every act begins in the mind before it is actually committed. Thus in dealing with the sixth commandment: 'Thou shalt not kill', Jesus declared that anger, abusive language, and contempt reveal inner attitudes which conduce to murder, and are equally to be condemned.

To look on a woman to lust after her is as sinful as the act of adultery itself: because adultery has already been committed in the imagination. Lust is an expression of man in his lowest state of delusion, when he identifies himself with his bodily sensations.

In order that the spiritual man may be allowed to develop without hindrance, instinctive physical habits must be ruthlessly curbed, even to the point of amputation: 'And if thy right eye offend thee, pluck it out and cast it from thee.' *Matthew* v.29.

In His interpretation of the Commandments, the aim of Jesus throughout was to eliminate as far as possible man's natural impulse to self-assertion, and to replace it with non-resistance. The claims and rights of the separate self or ego are everywhere reduced to nothing. Rather than resist or hate another, it is better to accept force and injustice with docility. Hatred and persecution should be met with love and forgiveness.

To accept this teaching is to accept the doctrine of impersonality, to acquire the habit of viewing every occurrence with an impersonal detachment entirely free from self-concern. This is the Way of Perfection, the perfection of the Universal Life Force or God the Father, which grants the blessings of life freely to all, irrespective of individual merit.

Jesus also drew attention to the fact of Change and Imper-

nanence, and warned against devoting one's life to the accumu-
ation of treasures subject to decay and dissolution. Only spiri-
ual truth, safely lodged in the heart, is immune from the un-
:easing inroads of Change; this treasure cannot be stolen, and
ibides for ever. A deep insight into the fact of Change and Im-
)ermanence will create an inner attitude of non-attachment to
naterial possessions.

In discussing man's inner attitude, Jesus stressed the import-
ince of single-mindedness. One cannot be in a state of self-
ielusion and of true insight at one and the same time. 'The light
)f the body is the eye (i.e. the consciousness): if therefore thine
:ye be single, thy whole body shall be full of light. But if thine
:ye be evil (i.e. in a state of delusion) thy whole body shall be
full of darkness. If therefore the light that is in thee be darkness
'i.e. self-delusion) how great is that darkness.' *Matthew* vi.22,
'3.

The Pharisees were trying to combine worldliness with reli-
;ion, the worship of mammon with the worship of God. The
worship of mammon is self-worship, which being entirely ex-
:lusive, separates man from his fellow-men and from God. This
:xclusive self-love must inevitably lead to hatred of everything
hat is not-self.

Anxiety about material and physical well-being, the main
:ause of greed and avarice should, therefore, be avoided, and be
·eplaced by an unswerving reliance upon God as the sure pro-
/ider of all man's real needs.

Jesus warned his hearers against judgment and criticism of
)thers, because they reveal an inner attitude of separation and
)f condemnation which is contagious, and will draw upon those
vho condemn others a similar condemnation. It is far better to
:urn one's attention upon one's own shortcomings. The humility
:hat shrinks from judging others, and is aware of its own im-

perfections, is the only attitude that allows for spiritual growth and development.

At the same time, while avoiding criticism and condemnation one must be able to discriminate between those who have developed spiritual discernment and those who have not. Some who have the appearance of men are still animals in human form. They are the dogs and the swine of whom Jesus spoke when He said: 'Give not that which is holy unto the dogs, neither cast ye your pearls before swine, lest they trample them under their feet, and turn again and rend you.' *Matthew* vii.6.

An essential part of the inner attitude must be faith in the efficacy of prayer. Everything that is good will be given to those who ask with the simplicity and confident expectancy of a child turning to his earthly father. But there is a Law of Reciprocity which must be observed, since man is often the instrument of God's good-will. We set a limit to the mutual interaction of benevolence by our own inner attitude: what we give to others will be given to us, and what we withhold from others will be withheld from us. 'Therefore, all things whatsoever ye would that men should do to you, do ye even so to them: for this is the law and the prophets.' *Matthew* vii.12.

Jesus compares the inner attitude of the mind to a gate which opens on to a way or road: the gate of self-delusion and the gate of self-denial. The first is wide and leads to a broad way, the other is strait and leads to a narrow way. The road of self-delusion is the obvious, the easy, way, and leads to destruction whereas the narrow way of self-denial leads to life. According to Jesus, few take the narrow way, the way of self-denial, but many choose the way of self-delusion.

The inner attitude can be changed by suggestions and ideas from outside. That is why every teaching must be carefully tested, to see whether it be true or false. The validity of a new idea or teaching must be judged by its results. False doctrines can be clothed in fine words, but that only makes them the more dangerous and destructive.

The test of sincerity is obedience to the will of God. A regular and constant application of the principles set forth in the Sermon on the Mount is necessary for enduring spiritual growth: he who does so is compared to a wise man who builds his house upon a rock. Failure to put these principles into practice is to remain in the state of delusion, which is compared to a foolish man building his house upon the sand.

When the mind has reached the state of enlightenment which understands the nature of self-delusion, the inner attitude based on such an understanding would naturally express itself more and more in the type of conduct advocated by Jesus. The re-nunciation of self-delusion cannot fail to be followed by self-denial. But until that stage of enlightenment is reached, the only alternative is the practice of self-denial itself as an act of obedi-ence to the Will of God.

To accept obedience to the Will of God as an essential con-dition of right thought and action is to form a new inner attitude which will transform self-assertion into humility and grace. So that without a complete understanding of the nature of self-delusion, repeated acts of self-denial performed in the spirit of obedience will bring some of the benefits of enlightenment.

The full benefit of enlightenment cannot be received while there remains any conflict between the self and God. Even when self-delusion is restrained in the spirit of obedience, it is still there, ever striving to assert itself, and until it is utterly de-stroyed, man is not free.

To follow Christ, or to enter the state of complete self-identification with the Universal Mind, there must be formed an attitude of non-attachment to places and to people. 'And

Jesus said unto him, The foxes have holes, and the birds of the air have nests, but the Son of man hath not where to lay his head.' *Matthew* viii.20. 'Follow me, and let the dead bury their dead.' *Matthew* viii.22.

Spiritual enlightenment is the result of reflection on the facts of individual experience, the fruit of this reflection giving rise to new attitudes of mind, which in turn provide new interpretations of experience.

The attitude of humble obedience to the Will of God which accepts certain forms of self-denial will result in a deeper experience of humility, so that the attitude of obedience will gradually change into the attitude of humility. A prolonged acquaintance with humility brings a tranquillity unknown to the self-assertive, a more enduring joy than the satisfaction of self-will. With the growth of humility as a consistent inner attitude of mind there will grow a deeper insight into the nature of experience: it will be seen as a reflection of man's own desire.

Self-will and self-assertion involve men more and more in the consequences of action intended to direct the course of events in accordance with individual desire. One of the benefits of humility is a passive indifference or detachment which removes the impulse to action.

The humble also learns the wisdom of silence, for speech is one of the chief instruments of self-assertion. It is a form of action which becomes the cause of further action. By refraining from unnecessary speech, the humble avoids becoming involved in pointless activities, and in ill-considered courses of action. Being humble, he does not fritter away his energies in idle talk, but listens in silence to the voice within his own being.

The attitude of humility resulting in detachment and the love of silence provides an opportunity for the growth of the powers of observation and reflection. A deeper insight into the causes of human suffering will be acquired, and with insight will come a new attitude of compassion.

The self or ego cannot survive unless its needs and claims remain constantly in the focus of consciousness. As compassion grows deeper and more inclusive, the self is pushed into the background: its grip is weakened, and the ego-delusion gradually disintegrates. Thus, even without a clear understanding of the ego-delusion, its power can be considerably reduced by the regular practice of obedience and humility.

It is not possible to practice obedience and humility for any length of time in isolation: there must be an awareness of someone in whose presence we must be humble, and whom we desire to obey, an ideal figure who combines within himself all the qualities to which the mind is attracted in this stage of development. The reality of this ideal figure in consciousness becomes the source of inspiration and an object of love.

This inner attitude is the attitude of discipleship: the seeker after Truth becomes a disciple of Jesus Christ.

12

Learn of Me

THE disciple is one who desires to learn, and to understand perfect knowledge. In the state of self-delusion there is only the relative knowledge of good and evil, of personal desire and aversion, of greed and hatred. In this condition of darkest ignorance, man is not aware that there is anything else to be known.

To withdraw deliberately from a world dominated by self-assertion and self-seeking requires great strength of purpose and unassailable convictions. The insidious influence of the world can be counteracted only by the example of One who overcame the world. 'These things I have spoken unto you, that in me ye might have peace. In the world ye shall have tribulation: but be of good cheer: I have overcome the world.' *John* xvi.33.

By the words 'in the world', Jesus meant the world of human delusion, a self-created world based on ignorance, which by reason of its unreality, is bound to be the source of tribulation. By overcoming the world, one overcomes the delusion on which it is based. The disciple who obeys the commandments, and follows the example of Jesus, builds for himself a new world whose foundation is self-denial.

Self-denial must not be confused with an arid and sterile asceticism practised for its own sake: on the contrary, it must be regarded as the essential condition of spiritual growth and development. As obedience to the commandments becomes a habit, the amount of energy required to resist the forces of self-delusion will be reduced, and more energy will be available for higher forms of activity.

The earthly life of Jesus Christ provides a perfect pattern of fruitful activity: prayer, meditation, and good works. 'How God anointed Jesus of Nazareth with the Holy Ghost and with power: who went about doing good, and healing all that were oppressed of the devil; for God was with him.' *The Acts* x.38.

To confine oneself entirely to prayer and meditation would be to remain in the delusion of separation: withdrawal from the world must be balanced by 'going about doing good'. Every act of compassion induces a sense of unity with others, which brings its own reward of joy and peace. Every moment of self-forgetfulness is a moment of freedom.

'And ye shall know the truth, and the truth shall make you free ... If the Son therefore shall make you free, ye shall be free indeed.' *John* viii.31, 36.

The state of self-delusion, of a belief in a separate self or ego, is a state of bondage which finds expression in various forms of activity, and those activities lead to further entanglements in the world of human illusion. This inner servitude expresses itself outwardly as cravings of all kinds, as insatiable as they are futile, for they must all end in frustration and defeat.

The disciple who takes Jesus for his guide must study with the utmost diligence and care the utterances of the Master as they are recorded in the New Testament. Every word spoken by Him is pregnant with meaning, and nourishes the soul. 'The words that I speak unto you, they are spirit and they are life.' *John* vi.63.

Life for each one is composed of a number of ideas held in consciousness, and from these ideas an interpretation of, or an attitude towards life is formed. Any trace of the delusion of a separate, independent ego involves the mind in self-concern and in attachment to the world of the senses.

The ideas contained in the sayings of Jesus cannot be acted

upon without self-denial, a process of dissolving the great mass of accumulated states of consciousness formed by desire and aversion in the past, and which has crystallized into what is regarded as the 'self', or 'personality'. To obey the commandments of Jesus, this 'self' must be completely ignored; it must be treated as of no account: as if, in fact, it had no real existence.

To learn of Jesus is to throw all past accumulated states of consciousness, all previous conceptions governed or formed by self-delusion, upon the scrap-heap. It is to start afresh, with a new mind and a new purpose. The new mind is open and receptive, ready to experiment with new ideas, willing to grow and to expand; the new purpose: to overcome the self-created world of desire and aversion.

When self-denial is achieved, even for only a short while, there comes a sense of pure consciousness, of unconditioned being, in which there is neither good nor evil, but only peace and harmony. There is no resistance to persons or conditions; there is no desire to manipulate or to change events to one's own advantage. There is acceptance and detachment.

If we remain long enough in a state of acceptance and detachment, we become dimly aware of an inner being within us, who dwells there in secret, about whom we know nothing. Yet this inner being has always been within us. Constant attention to the reactions of the conscious mind to the visible world of the five senses, and the identification of these reactions with a permanent 'self' or ego, produce a limited and superficial state of consciousness which, for those who remain in it, constitutes this world.

The main purpose of the teachings of Jesus was to destroy that world, to break up that state of consciousness. Crucifixion is a symbol of self-denial. To follow Jesus and to be His disciple, all the claims of the false self must be abandoned, and every form of self-assertion renounced. Good-will must replace resentment and retaliation. A consistent application of these principles will gradually remove the veils of self-delusion, and reveal the inner man. 'If any man serve me, let him follow me; where I am, there shall also my servant be.' *John* xii.26.

The inner man is content to be a servant. His joy is to be of service to others, for love is the very essence of his being. To become aware of the inner man is to be in contact with the Universal Spirit which animates all flesh.

Self-denial cannot be practised in isolation: it can only be practised in our relationships with other people. It is the existence of other people and the demands they make upon us, that makes possible the choice between self-assertion and self-denial. 'But I say unto you which hear, Love your enemies, do good to them which hate you, Bless them which curse you, and pray for them which despitefully use you.' *Luke* vi.27, 28.

This choice has constantly to be made, and when the right choice is taken, the practice of self-denial becomes a habit. Thus the unpleasant behaviour of others is a means of grace, and human society a school for spiritual growth. Our enemies are our friends in disguise, for without them we would not have the opportunity to rise high enough above the self to be able to love them. Those who hate us do us great service, for without them we could not overcome hatred in order to do good to them. Every unfortunate or evil encounter becomes a means of grace and an opportunity for self-mastery.

Events which otherwise would have been labelled good or evil, become for the disciple of Christ milestones on the road to freedom from the bondage of desire and aversion. He overcomes his greatest enemy: himself; and having overcome himself, he conquers all.

More than this, he overcomes the past, for every action he is called upon to forgive has already occurred. By loving his enemies, by blessing those who curse him, the disciple refuses to dwell on what is past, and it has no dominion over his mind. His consciousness is not cluttered up with memories of hostility or curses. He meets enmity with good-will, and anger with tolerance and understanding.

To withdraw from the arena of self-assertion is to avoid the fatigue of futile conflicts, and of useless activities. He becomes aware of a consciousness free of conflict, free of desire and aversion. He becomes pure consciousness, in which there is awareness without self-reference. This awareness of what flows into the stream of consciousness, although impersonal as far as any self-reference is concerned, is not devoid of feeling. There is, on the contrary, a sense of unity, of joy, and of love.

The Universal Spirit of Life is the Father, and the Christ or the Son is the consciousness of the Spirit, and the Essence of that consciousness is Joy and Love. The disciple who enters into that state of consciousness by means of self-denial becomes the servant of that Spirit of Joy and Love.

Before the disciple can enter into that state of consciousness, there must be a cleansing of the subconscious mind or the heart, as it is called in the Bible: 'Keep thy heart with all diligence, for out of it are the issues of life.' *Proverbs* iv.23. 'The heart is deceitful above all things, and desperately wicked; who can know it?' *Jeremiah* xvii.9. In the subconscious mind lie deep-rooted habits of thought, and a long-standing attitude of which the conscious mind may not be aware. 'For from within, out of the heart of men, proceed evil thoughts . . .' *Mark* vii.21. In 1 Peter iii.4, we find an apt description of the subconscious mind: 'the hidden man of the heart.'

No matter what principles of behaviour the conscious mind may accept, they must be deeply felt before they will make any impression on the hidden man of the heart. Such an inner conversion comes sometimes after a period of remorse, or sorrow or adversity. 'Now for a long season Israel hath been without the true God, and without a teaching priest, and without law ... And in those times there was no peace to him that went out, nor to him that came in, but great vexations were upon all the inhabitants of the countries ... And they entered into a covenant to seek the Lord God of their fathers with all their heart and with all their soul.' 2 *Chronicles* xv.3, 5, 12.

To learn of Jesus Christ is to come under the spell of His character and personality as the embodiment of the perfection of the spiritual life; it is to become aware of His Presence whenever the self is completely denied: and in that Presence is peace. 'Peace I leave with you, my peace I give unto you: not as the world giveth, give I unto you'. *John* xiv.27.

Whatever the world gives, it demands something in return, because it is ruled by desire. The Christ, being pure consciousness devoid of self-awareness, has no needs and is without desire.

The negative practice of self-denial becomes the positive practice of pure consciousness, in which the disciple strives to achieve a state of consciousness into which the ego-concept does not obtrude, in which there is awareness without self-reference or self-concern. In the state of delusion the mind reflects the light of consciousness continually upon sense-reactions and their emotions from which springs the ceaseless alternation of desire and aversion.

Whenever the mind is able to withdraw the reflected light of consciousness from the outer world and its reactions to it, then it becomes aware of the life-consciousness itself. The curtain of illusion is drawn back and the door of consciousness is open. 'Behold, I stand at the door and knock; if any man hear my voice, and open the door, I will come in to him, and will sup with him, and he with me.' *Revelation* iii.20.

13

I Am the Door

In the Holy Scriptures, 'I AM' is an expression of the deepest significance. It was revealed to Moses as the name of God. 'And Moses said unto God, Behold, when I come unto the children of Israel, and shall say unto them, The God of your fathers hath sent me unto you; and they shall say to me, What is his name? What shall I say unto them? And God said unto Moses, I AM THAT I AM: Thus shalt thou say unto the children of Israel, I AM hath sent me unto you.' *Exodus* iii.13, 14.

In other words, God is the conscious Life wherever and in whatever form it manifests itself. It is Life aware of itself as a centre of consciousness. 'In him was life and the life was the light of men.' *John* i.3. Consciousness is an attribute of life, and wherever there is life, there is some degree of consciousness.

The whole purpose of self-denial is the expansion and enlargement of consciousness, so that its light may penetrate and disperse the mists of illusion. Jesus said: 'I am the door: by me if any man enter in, he shall be saved, and shall go in and out, and find pasture.' *John* x.9. The door is the door of consciousness: it is the door which must be opened if man is to escape from the darkness of self-delusion.

Progress depends on individual faith and effort. 'Ask, and it shall be given you; seek and ye shall find; knock, and it shall be opened unto you.' *Matthew* vii.7. Delusion is the thief that robs man of true understanding. 'The thief cometh not, but for to steal, and to kill, and to destroy. I am come that they might have life, and they might have it more abundantly.' *John* x.10.

The self-centred mind is full of negative thoughts born of self-concern: and these negative thoughts rob him of joy, and destroy his peace of mind.

The true state of consciousness Jesus compares to the shepherd of the sheep, which are the innocent thoughts of what is good. He compares all previous states of consciousness to thieves and robbers. 'All that ever came before me are thieves and robbers; but the sheep did not hear them.' *John* x.8.

Jesus Christ is the embodiment of the highest state of spiritual consciousness. 'I am the good shepherd: the good shepherd giveth his life for the sheep.' This state cannot be reached until the life of the senses, of self-assertion, of ego-delusion, has been renounced and sacrificed.

The disciple must picture his conscious mind as a shepherd whose flock is ideas, and in order that ideas of good may thrive, he must sacrifice all negative thoughts, and so lead his flock of innocent thoughts to 'the green pastures and the still waters'.

The Universal Life, which Jesus calls the Father, dwells in man. All that is not of the Father springs from the deluded human mind which identifies itself with sense-impressions and sense-reactions. 'For all that is in the world, the lust of the flesh, and the lust of the eyes, and the pride of life, is not of the Father, but is of the world.' 1 *John* ii.16.

The man in the state of self-delusion is compared to a servant, because he is not in control of his mind. He is at the mercy of his sense-reactions. 'But he that is an hireling, and not the shepherd, whose own the sheep are not, seeth the wolf coming, and leaveth the sheep, and fleeth; and the wolf catcheth them, and scattereth the sheep.' *John* x.12.

The wolf stands for the fears and anxieties that continually beset the unillumined mind.

When the mind is truly enlightened, it becomes the instrument of spiritual consciousness. Everything exists within a man's own consciousness, and by mastery of the mind, it is possible to focus its light consistently on that which is good. 'And when he was demanded of the Pharisees when the kingdom of God should come, he answered them and said, The kingdom of God cometh not with observation. Neither shall they say, Lo, here! or, Lo, there! for, behold, the kingdom of God is within you.' *Luke* xvii.20, 21.

Spiritual consciousness is the consciousness of the Life which is in man, and all around him. The qualities of this consciousness are revealed in the Sermon on the Mount, and indeed in almost every saying of Jesus about humility, forgiveness, non-resistance to evil, and impersonal love. These are the attributes of the Spirit, impersonal and unresisting, available to man in the Life that dwells within him and all around him. This Life is the servant of man, obedient to his slightest wish, accepting all his beliefs.

The docility of Life ensures man's freedom to do what he will, but since the essence of spiritual consciousness, i.e. the consciousness of Life, is love and harmony, the delusions of man produce disharmony and suffering. 'I am the way, the truth, and the life: no man cometh unto the Father but by me.' *John* xiv.6.

Self-denial is, therefore, the abandonment of the delusion of a separate, independent ego or self; it is the recognition of the life within with its own consciousness of love, joy and harmony, as the truth of individual being; it is to allow the life within its fullest possible expression in all circumstances. 'Know ye not that ye are the temple of God, and that the Spirit of God dwelleth in you?' I *Corinthians* iii.16.

Jesus made this clear when He said: 'Believest thou not that I am in the Father and the Father in me? the words that I

87

speak unto you, I speak not of myself: but the Father, that dwelleth in me, he doeth the works.' *John* xiv.10.

The same truth is expressed by Paul: 'I am crucified with Christ: nevertheless I live; yet not I, but Christ liveth in me.' *Galatians* ii.20. By crucifixion, he means self-denial, or the death of the ego-delusion, by which alone the emergence of the Spirit of Christ into consciousness is made possible.

Crucifixion is followed by a resurrection: as the old state of mortal consciousness recedes, the new state of spiritual consciousness is unveiled. 'Jesus said unto her, I am the resurrection and the life; he who believeth on me, though he were dead, yet shall he live.' *John* xi.25.

This, then, is the paradox of self-denial: that true happiness can be found only by those who do not seek it, that fulness of life comes only with the death of self, that abundance is for those who ask for nothing. Without desire or aversion, without greed or hatred, man sets himself free to enter that state of consciousness which is revealed in Jesus as the universal love and compassion of the One Eternal Life, and, uniting himself with that Life, he rises above Time and circumstance into the Kingdom of God.